GINTER

Jan-Udo Wenzel

The Caitlin Press
Prince George, British Columbia
1993

The Caitlin Press
P.O. Box 2387, Station B
Prince George, B.C. V2N 2S6
Canada

The Caitlin Press would like to acknowledge the financial support of the Canada Council and British Columbia Cultural Fund.

Canadian Cataloguing in Publication Data

Wenzel, Jan-Udo, 1938-
  Ginter

Includes Index.
ISBN 0-920576-35-4

  1. Ginter, Ben. 2. Businessmen—British Columbia—Biography.
3. Real estate developers —British Columbia—Biography.
4. Prince George (B.C.)—Biography. I. Title.
HC112.5.G55W45 1992   338'.04'092   C92-091507-8

Cover Design by Roger Handling
Typeset in Stempel Garamond by Vancouver Desktop Publishing Centre
Printed in Canada

Acknowledgements

I wish to acknowledge and thank the following persons for their special contributions to the book: My friends Jim Stirling and Pete Miller; Tom Leboe, Stan McKay and Jim Hubbard of Pacific Western Brewery for their steadfast support over the years; Al McNair, Roy Nagel, Doug Martin, Kyle Storey, Bob Miller, Lee Anderson, and Arnold Olson of *The Prince George Citizen*; Dave Milne, Lorne Lloyd, and Murray Swanson; my publishers Cynthia Wilson and Ken Carling; Chris Hansen; Paul Seens and Kathy Plett of the College of New Caledonia; Curley Oldach; Derek Tait who first suggested the project; Robert Harkins, local historian and friend; my oldest friends Bob Locker and Evelyn Eaglespeaker-Locker for their hospitality; former Ginter employees Louise McCormick, Walter Betcher, Uwe Aroe, and many others too numerous to mention here by name but whose contributions I value; my friends John Steinhofer and Henry Lielich; the staff of the Fraser Fort George Regional Museum; past and present officials of the International Brotherhood of Operating Engineers, Local 115; pioneer union agent Howard German; Mel Rothenburger and Peter Vander Lielee of *The Kamloops Daily News*; my daughter Kerstin for teaching me how to use the word processor; former Ginter executives Joe Rinaldi and Henry Binder; BC Rail for providing travel. And a special thank you to Mrs. Grace Ginter.

The author gratefully acknowledges the support of Mr. Myron Sambad, president of Bater Electric (1983) Ltd. of Prince George in the making of this book.

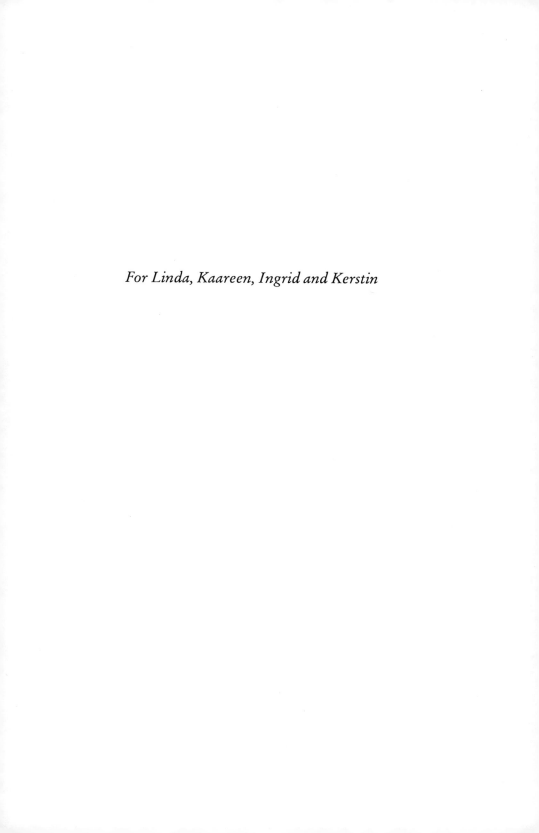

For Linda, Kaareen, Ingrid and Kerstin

Preface

A motorist travelling along the highways of British Columbia will likely drive his car on a road originally built by Benjamin George Ginter. A shopper using a kraft paper bag could presumably use one made from paper produced by Eurocan Pulp and Paper in Kitimat, another one of many enterprises started by the same man. While beer made in Prince George is now brewed by Pacific Western Brewing Company Limited, it was Ben Ginter who revived the art of brewing in the North.

Ginter played a large role in the development of the province and his name was familiar to many throughout British Columbia. He happened to be the right man in the right place at the right time. At the height of his career, he employed almost ten thousand people, no small feat in the 1950s and 1960s for a one-man operator.

He came from humble beginnings. He rode the rails in the Dirty Thirties. He worked long and hard, and through this work he rose to the top. He was beholden to no man and he knew it, but this knowledge also bred arrogance and a certain contempt for others who were not as strong as he was.

And yet today, hardly a trace of his name can be found in public. There is no street or building named after him in his chosen town of Prince George. When his name is mentioned today it is more often than not used in a derogatory way. The famous doggerel "Ginter, Gaglardi and God" has aged into a joke. To many people the memory of Ben Ginter is not a happy one. Many he had fired or had taken to court. Others had to take him to court and felt his wrath. Yet others believed and still believe that Ben Ginter was one of the greatest men who ever lived because he was straight with them.

Ben Ginter was a controversial man when he was alive, and he remains so more than a decade after his death. People either admired him, saying he was a great man, or hated him, saying he was the biggest scoundrel that ever lived in the North. It was Ginter, more than anyone else before or since, who put Prince George and the North in the spotlight. It was Ginter, not mayors and councils past or present, who informed the rest of Canada of a city called Prince George and of an enormously open country waiting to be developed and to be discovered. It was Ginter who showed the rest of the province that there was life beyond Hope, life worth living.

This story is by necessity incomplete. There were at one time almost ten thousand people working for him and I am sure there are almost ten thousand stories circulating today. I could not get all of them but hope that those I did get will convey an accurate picture of one of British Columbia's most colourful men. Some people may also feel the story is incomplete as it does not go too deeply into the influences others may have had on Ginter and his actions. But remember, this is the story of Ben Ginter; everyone else is just a bit player.

Regardless of how anyone may feel about Ben Ginter, the truth is he was a mover, and he worked his way into British Columbia's history. There was nothing he could not do once he made up his mind. He was not afraid of anyone. How many people can say, as individuals, that they will build a $100 million pulp mill? How many would be willing to tangle with one of the great oligopolies in this country, the national beer barons? And how many would even dream of tackling such mega-risks such as bidding $12 million for timber rights while his competitors offered only $340,000?

There's no doubt, Ben Ginter thought big, lived big and played big: he was a big man.

How good a man he was, I will leave up to the readers.

— Jan-Udo Wenzel
Prince George, BC
Summer 1993

On the morning of January 29, 1976 three men walked into the compound of Ben Ginter Construction Company Limited in Prince George, British Columbia and took over operation of an empire. It was not an illegal takeover or even a sinister one. On the contrary, these men represented the law, but their action eventually ended in the destruction of the Ginter Group of industries and indirectly in the death of Ben Ginter himself . . .

1

BENJAMIN GEORGE GINTER, son of Teofil and Henrietta, was born February 10, 1923 and always claimed he had been born in Swan River, Manitoba. However, his family had settled in Canada in 1929, thereby making it impossible for Ben Ginter to have been born in this country.

The naturalization papers of Teofil Ginter illustrate an interesting chapter in European history. Ben Ginter's father's birth place is near the city of Wolyn in Russia. His brother Fred was also born in Russia, but Ben and his sisters were born in Poland. The family didn't move; the border did. Poland attacked the Soviets following the First World War and annexed some of the lands belonging to the Ukraine and Byelorussia. Wolyn was in one of the disputed regions. The Ginters were members of a German Baptist community which suffered economic hardship and religious discrimination at the hands of the Polish Catholic invaders. They and many others in their Baptist community emigrated to Canada in the 1920s.

For most of his life, Ben Ginter successfully maintained that he was born in Manitoba. When he applied for a Canadian passport in 1960, he claimed citizenship because he was a "native-born

Canadian. While the passport lists the year of his birth as 1923, the naturalization papers of his father, which gave Teofil, Ben, and his three foreign-born siblings Canadian citizenship, state Ben was born in 1922.

Once in Canada, the family settled on a farm in Minitonas, a small community east of Swan River, Manitoba. The farm consisted of a quarter section of land or 160 acres. Before the Ginters could make a living, they had to clear prairie bush. Every family member had to do his or her share in raising the crops, a few cattle, chickens, as well as maintaining a garden. Life was not easy, Ben recalled sometimes, but all had enough to eat. According to Ben, his mother Henrietta was the driving force in the family.

Ginter probably chose Swan River to call his birthplace to save himself a lot of explanations. It also allowed him to escape the stigma of being foreign-born. At the time feelings in the Prairies were still strong against East Europeans, even though a large number of the Prairie settlers were foreign-born immigrants including fellow Baptists who also settled in the Minitonas area. Saying that he had been born in Manitoba was much easier than explaining that he had been born in a place no one had ever heard of.

Ben Ginter went to school at Rolling River, a close-by community. When Ben was in Grade Eight, he left school because his father had died. This was all the formal schooling Ginter was ever to receive. In later years any story written about him included this fact, sometimes in admiration, but more often it was to point out that he was not as well educated as, and thereby less acceptable, than others who had more formal schooling. However, Ginter learned to use this lack of schooling as a weapon in his rise. While he sometimes openly regretted not having had a better formal education, at other times he pointed out that it was possible for anyone to rise above his beginnings despite this lack as long as he had enough drive and stamina to succeed.

Those who knew him well are certain that the feelings of inferiority he tried to hide, but which were obvious to close observers, were caused by his lack of formal education. The result was not necessarily a negative thing. Indeed, it became his motivation to always be better than anyone else at whatever he tried. He became an overachiever. His feeling of inferiority seems to be the root of his often abrasive and sometimes downright rude behavior to people who worked for him. After Ginter made it to the top he often delighted in ordering people around and making them feel inadequate, especially if these employees were university graduates or held professional certificates. He often put these people "in their places" as he called it. Ordering them around served as a booster for his own ego and reduced any of his envy and/or fear of their education to a level he could handle.

As further evidence of his feelings of inferiority, Ginter never established long-lasting friendships. Even relations with his siblings were fragile. His brother Fred, who moved to Prince George when Ben was well established, did not get along with Ben. "They got into each other's hair almost every time they got together," said a nephew.

Their enmity could have been rooted in an episode in their youth. Shortly before World War II, Fred Ginter, a few years older than his brother, owned a stallion. He travelled around

Manitoba charging stud fees for his animal's services. Most farmers would delay payment until after a foal was born. That meant Fred Ginter had money coming in, but he joined the army before he could collect most of it. Also on the farm in Minitonas sat a Model T Ford which belonged to Fred. With Fred in the army, Ben bought a new battery for the vehicle and drove it as if it were his own. He also collected the stud fees from the farmers, but did not bank the money for his soldier brother. Ben used it for himself. Later, when Ben was rich, Ben paid Fred back — with interest. Fred never again trusted his brother, and all business dealings between the two were handled on a cash basis.

When the Ginter children left home, they spread out across the country. After Ben had become rich and famous, he hosted two family reunions, paying all transportation costs. These meetings served to rebuild family relations, which had been rather loose mostly due to geography. Ben was not without his generous side, especially when it reflected well on him.

Even early on, Ben Ginter had all the makings of a workaholic, and over the years developed into one. He would rise very early in the morning and have a cup of coffee. He would be the first one at the office. During the day Ginter did not eat unless he was meeting someone. When he had no meetings, he would work during lunch hours and long into the nights. He made telephone calls, met with employees, surveyed plans, and checked on the progress of his projects. Late at night he would have a hearty meal, which — if he had his way — would be steak and onions or spaghetti.

When everyone else had gone home, Ginter would still be at his desk. Finally leaving the office, he usually would take some work home. In later years when there was no one waiting for him, Ginter would keep working in his hotel suite. He would review the previous day, and if there were any questions in his mind, he would pick up the telephone and call the person responsible. It did not matter what time of night it was; Ginter would call and discuss work. This habit would stay with him to the end of his life.

With people who worked with their hands, Ginter acted differently. Here he was on safe ground and could stop pretending to be something he was not. Said one long-time employee, "Ben was always a cat-skinner at heart."

Jim Hubbard who worked for Ginter for many years in many places and capacities said Ginter would get along well with people who were straightforward and truthful with him. "If you lied to him and he found out — even years later — he would confront you and you got fired," Hubbard said. He added Ginter also took an interest in the families of those he liked and trusted. He would even come over for a meal. "I think Mr. Ginter was one of the few rich men who had time for a working man and I will always appreciate him for that."

Hubbard worked for Ginter in Red Deer, Alberta, as well as in Prince George. They travelled several times by car between the two cities, and Hubbard said Ginter would talk with him about his life, his interests, and hobbies. He recalls Ginter as a straightforward, honest man who looked after those he took a liking to.

As an example Hubbard pointed out the time when he wanted to buy a house in Red Deer, but did not have the money. Ginter told him to go to the bank and borrow the money and he, Ginter, would back him up. Hubbard did and a telephone call to Ginter by the bank manager resulted in the immediate issuance of a cheque for the amount requested. The papers were taken care of later. Hubbard said that when he left the brewery with Ginter after a day's work, they rarely talked about business. Ginter was fond of shooting pool with Hubbard at the Red Deer Legion hall. "He was just like anyone else there. He bought a round, I bought a round. There never was a thought given to him being a million-aire and me being his employee," Hubbard said.

Ginter was thirteen years old when he left school and for another year he stayed around the farm, which was now run by his mother. Then he struck out on his own. He never liked to talk much about those years, but he was proud of having ridden the rails east to Ontario where he stacked logs, worked on farms, and laboured as well in construction. He would return to the family farm to visit, but never lived there again for any length of time.

"I always sent my money home to my mother to help her with my brothers and sisters and with the farm," Ginter was fond of saying when he was in a reflective mood. Asked what he lived on if he sent his earnings home, Ginter would smile and say, "I played poker and supported myself quite well."

If true — and there is no reason for it not to be — this was no small feat because it was the tail end of the Great Depression and Ben was still a teenager. In Winnipeg, he met Henry Binder, a fellow Minitonian, whom he had known as a boy. Binder had come to Winnipeg to see a city for the first time. Both were looking for a job and had heard there were jobs open hauling logs in the Fort William area in Ontario, but getting to Fort William cost money and both men were short. Binder said Ginter engaged other waiting travellers in a poker game while he watched out for the train. When the train arrived, Ben had won enough to buy two tickets to Fort William. So began a relationship which lasted for many years.

There were thousands of unemployed roaming the country trying to find work. At the height of what became known as the Great Depression, Canadian unemployment reached twenty-three per cent. It was not until William Lyon Mackenzie King, whose Liberals ousted the ineffective Conservatives of Richard B. Bennett in 1935, adopted programs similar to those of President Franklin Delano Roosevelt to battle the depression in the United States that life improved in Canada.

Ginter never forgot those years and later he stated that "even a million dollar inheritance does not ensure success. You've got to know what it is like to be without. You have to know how to perform to appreciate the value of money and work and respon-sibility." The first years on his own were his years "without" for Ginter who worked at any job he could get. He moulded tires, cut and loaded logs, but always returned to construction work. Over the years he worked himself up to master mechanic, foreman, and construction supervisor.

Ginter did not join the Armed Forces, although Canada was at war with Germany by this time. He always maintained he was performing work vital to the Canadian war effort. During those years there was plenty of work for anyone willing to work hard, and Ginter never shied away from hard work.

When the war was over, he married Grace Myrtle Peraux on

September 8, 1945 in Lethbridge, Alberta. Ginter was twenty-three years old at the time and his bride was sixteen. Ben and Grace had met about five months earlier. A girl-friend of Grace's was going out with a fellow from Minitonas who knew Ben Ginter. They double-dated on several occasions and Ben seemed to be so smitten with this new girl that he proposed marriage after only a few dates. Grace, however, held out for five months. Was it love that persuaded her to marry this brassy young man? "Every young girl dreams of getting married and I was no exception," Grace Ginter recalled years later.

Ben had to borrow the twenty-five dollar fee for the marriage from a friend and the new Mrs. Ginter paid for the ring. She had been working as a nurse's aide at St. Michael's Catholic Hospital. Despite her French maiden name, Grace was of Irish-Swedish descent, and the Ginter wedding was held at her Swedish grandparents' place in Lethbridge. The name Peraux was that of her stepfather.

There was no honeymoon because there was no money, and the couple returned to a construction camp. "We moved into a trailer and slept at one end, and the crews slept in the other end," Grace said.

Ben was employed as a Cat operator, and he got his new wife a job as the camp cook. Construction camps were to be the homes of the newly-weds for several years. When Ginter started to work for himself, Grace Ginter cooked for the men her husband hired to work for him, and she looked after Ben's books. Grace Ginter liked to follow her husband from job to job and said she never missed staying in one place.

Even if there were no honeymoon, the Ginters later travelled a lot. Ben liked going to Florida and Mexico and always seemed to

Ben and Grace Ginter pose for their official wedding photo,
September 8, 1945.

Ben and Grace entertain friends at a formal dinner in Las Vegas on one of their first trips to Vegas.

have a good time. Grace Ginter said he was a person who always needed a crowd around him and had no problem making new friends. Wherever the Ginters travelled, Ben would meet someone in the hotel or a bar; he would take a liking to this person who then would become part of the Ginters' vacation.

Once in Florida they met an American couple, and when Ben found out it took less than an hour to go to Cuba, he invited the newly-found friends to go along. From his days of riding the rails Ben loved to gamble, and now that he could afford it, he indulged freely. It developed into a life-long habit. Why not? He had the

Playing the slots. Grace Ginter tries her luck in the casinos in Las Vegas on one of their frequent trips to Nevada's gambling capital.

money and he enjoyed himself. Ben would take off with his new-found friends and leave his wife to herself.

In Acapulco, Mexico, someone stole Ben's camera. Grace Ginter said she believed the local police department would never be the same. She said Ben made life difficult for the Mexican police by insisting they look for his camera and suspend all other business. The police at first did not take much notice of this tourist from Canada, but they had not counted on Ginter's way of doing things. He ended up riding a jeep with a Mexican police officer looking and searching through the slums and everywhere Ginter could think of. Despite all efforts, Ginter's camera was never found.

In Mexico, the Ginters, centre, make new friends as was Ben's custom on his trips.

Ben always enjoyed himself on their trips. He was willing to learn how to dance local dances such as the hula in Hawaii. He loved to show off his dancing skill and was pleased when others complimented him. The people he met on those trips were easily caught up in Ben's enthusiasm for everything. Once he had begun doing something he enjoyed, like dancing, he would shut the place down, outlasting Grace and his friends by hours.

Ben Ginter, centre front, learns the national dance in Hawaii on an early visit to the Islands. Other Prince Georgians were in the party.

2

In 1948, GINTER MET NOEL SMITH, a former Missouri farmer, in Alberta and with Smith's backing, Ginter went into business. Smith had moved to Saskatchewan and opened an equipment dealership in Saskatoon. Earlier in the year Ben Ginter had hitch-hiked from Alberta to Saskatoon to buy his first piece of machinery. He bought a scraper from Smith. Looking back, Smith, in his eighties now, recalled the lean young man covered with road dust walking onto his lot. He looked each piece over, and Smith could see the man knew what he was doing. So they started a conversation and since it was getting late, Smith invited Ginter to spend the night. Talking over a drink after business hours, Smith became certain Ginter had a good future. They discussed the construction business, and next day Ginter bought the scraper with money his mother lent him. Smith and Ginter would continue their associations into the 1960s when Ginter went into the beer brewing industry. Smith scouted the United States for the brewing equipment of bankrupt companies. It was the time of take-overs by the large American breweries which left many private brewers broke and willing to sell equipment.

Ginter and Smith first formed a construction company in 1948

Ben sits at the entrance of a trailer built by Grace's grandfather in downtown Prince George.

and worked for contractors throughout the Canadian West. Ben was good at his job and never lacked contracts. It was small stuff, he would say later. While Smith was willing to invest in a partnership, he insisted Ginter also put up some money. Ben did not have any money, and so he went to his mother for help. Henrietta lent him $1,500 for his share in the new venture. Ginter would never forget his mother's help and she always had a special place in her son's heart. Family ties figured in his hiring practice as one of his first employees was Walter Betcher, Ginter's sister Hilda's stepson.

In those early post war years, Canada was beginning to recover from the lingering effect of both the Great Depression and the war. Thousands of young men were coming home and hundreds of thousands of new immigrants were arriving. There was plenty of work.

The Ginters relaxing in their
first home in Prince George
around 1950.

By 1949 the province of British Columbia had joined the
development boom, and Ginter arrived in Prince George, a small
town located at the confluence of the Fraser and Nechako rivers,
almost in the geographical centre of the province, on November
11. It was a day Grace Ginter remembers well, because as soon as
they had checked into the hotel, she came down with the chicken
pox. The Ginters stayed at first in the downtown Columbus
Hotel. Then they moved to a trailer which Grace's grandfather
had built for eighty dollars. They were accompanied by Betcher.

Ben soon bought an army camp for $3,000. It was located on part
of the present-day Simon Fraser Hotel parking lot. In this army shed
Grace Ginter would cook for as many as thirty-five men. Grace
Ginter would be the first one up in the morning to make breakfast
for the men and the last one to go to bed because she still had to make
sandwiches for the morning shift. All this would be accomplished on
a wood stove. The Ginters later bought their first house at Fifth
Avenue and Winnipeg Street.

Ginter's arrival was later transformed into part of the mystique
surrounding him. He was quoted in several publications as saying:

"I came to Prince George with one machine, one pick-up, and one wife." As catchy as this may sound, it was not true. Ginter was sent to Prince George by a Winnipeg contractor, not as Ginter liked to say, "I chose Prince George because I could see it had a great future."

He arrived in Prince George with eight Cats and a grader. Shipping costs had been paid by the contractor, who later went out of business, leaving Ginter holding several bad cheques. But he had the machines and was ready to go to work. Prince George was nothing but a spot on the map of the province. It had no paved road connecting it to the rest of British Columbia and only one of the national railways passed through on its way from the Prairies to the West Coast. It was what anyone would call a hick town, although residents who had been living here for a while would get upset if anyone called their town a hick town. They still do. "We never were what you would call a hick town. Just imagine, anyone who lived here and belonged to a service club owned a tuxedo and his wife had at least one formal dress. We were conscious of living far away from the big city, but we maintained a certain level of culture here," said Wally West who arrived in Prince George in the early 1940s and started a successful photography business. The better element in the town was made up mostly of business-men and government employees who had formed several service clubs, established a library, and were constantly engaged in creat-ing a cultural climate. The other residents worked in sawmills and other "bush" jobs.

Aside from the occasional dressing up for a dance, Prince George offered little. The majority of its citizens were employed in the forest industry. The town had a reputation for being wild, as it still does. There were no sidewalks, except for a few wooden ones. Streets were not paved, and city hall was said to have been a house of ill repute at one time. A few hotels and two movie houses offered most of the public entertainment. There were less than 4,000 people living in this town, fewer than during the war when army units had been based there. Sawmills dotted the landscape around Prince George.

Prince George had been incorporated in 1915 when the Grand Trunk Pacific Railway came through on its way to the Pacific Ocean. The area had been the site of wild land speculations, and at one time there were four towns side by side: Fort George, Prince George, Central Fort George and South Fort George. All four sites hoped to be chosen the terminal for the railway's local station and yard. Grand Trunk Pacific chose Prince George to build its station on what was to become First Avenue. Prince George then merged with Central Fort George and Fort George, leaving out only South Fort George which remained independent until 1978. This was the Prince George Ben Ginter came to, and a few years later he put it on the map.

In the late 1940s, the provincial government in Victoria was trying to bring the Pacific Great Eastern Railway — now known as BC Rail — to Prince George, and Ginter was hired as a contractor to build track foundations. It was a steady job and Ginter performed well. His heavy equipment was busy at all times, and Ginter was making money. He was still in partnership with Noel Smith.

Ginter was working every waking hour. He had become obsessed with his jobs. He would later say he could see what kind of money he could make by simply working like everyone else.

Meat for the freezer — Ben
hunting moose in the early
1950s.

Being ambitious, he felt he could increase his efforts and thereby make far more money. Ginter also had a rare advantage. He had almost total recall of events, figures, and conversations. A former employee said Ginter could recall a conversation among several people almost verbatim a few weeks later and could point out contradictions and errors. This, combined with the drive to always be first, was an unbeatable combination when dealing with the competition.

It was the first time, he said, that his extra efforts were paying off in extraordinary returns. This always-making-the-extra-effort was to stay with him all his life. Many people thought he was too ambitious. They did their work and went home. If they were single, they might spent their earnings on booze and women, both in plentiful supply in Prince George. Not Ginter. He looked forward to bigger and better projects.

Ginter's unorthodox style spilled over into his hiring practice. If he needed someone on the spot, the first qualified applicant would get the job. A former cat-skinner recalls just arriving in Prince George after he had to leave Saskatchewan in a hurry. The man had some marital problems in the Prairies and wanted to get away, leaving behind a good job. He arrived in Prince George in his Sunday-best suit and went to see local relatives. Here he was told Ben Ginter was hiring, and the man went straight down to Ginter's office looking for a job. Ben Ginter happened to be at the compound and asked to see the man. He asked a few questions about the man's background. The Saskatchewan refugee supplied a telephone number for Ginter to check out the veracity of his statements and Ginter immediately called the number.

Ginter's face betrayed no emotions while he listened to the party on the other end of the line. He curtly thanked whoever he was speaking to and hung up. "Let's go," he told the job seeker.

"May I ask where we are going?" the man asked.

"To the job, you are hired," Ginter replied. They got into Ben's Thunderbird and Ben stepped on the gas. Some time later they arrived at the Pine Pass, some 200 kilometres north of Prince George. Two Cats were standing idle just off the road and Ginter pointed them out. "Come on, let's get to work," Ben said. The man hesitated. After all, he was hardly dressed for work. But, then, neither was Ginter. Noticing the reluctance, Ginter asked gruffly, "Do you want the job or not?" The man nodded and Ginter took him to the piece of machinery.

"You take this one and I'll take the other," Ben told his newest employee and both men worked until sundown. This rather unusual start of a working relationship resulted in a long-term job for the Saskatchewan man which ended only when Ginter's firm went out of business.

"I liked Ben as a boss. He knew what he was doing and could do the job himself, which was more than most other bosses could do. You could not pull the wool over his eyes," the now retired cat-skinner said.

Ginter had earned a reputation as a good performer on the jobs, and when the big Aluminium Company of Canada built its new smelter at Kitimat in 1953, Ginter was chosen to construct access roads. It is impossible to ascertain today how Ginter managed to get a contract with Alcan on such favorable terms. He supplied the machinery for the original Kemano project which included the building of the Kenny Dam to store water from the diverted Nechako River for Alcan's use in its smelter. The contract called for Ginter to be paid on an hourly basis whether his machines were working or not. If, for any reason work was halted, Ginter still was paid his rates, and he was able to turn a good profit from this job. It was a major project and laid the foundation of Ginter's future fortune. He formed Ben Ginter Construction Company (1953) Limited the same year. Ginter felt he now was ready to expand.

And, indeed, he won a contract from the federal government to build Baldy Hughes, a radar base near Prince George. Similar radar stations were spread out across Canada at the height of the Cold War to spot incoming Russian missiles and report them to NORAD headquarters in Colorado. Ginter also was hired to perform maintenance work after the station was completed.

3

In 1952 THE SOCIAL CREDIT PARTY OF BRITISH COLUMBIA ousted the Liberal-Conservative coalition government in Victoria. William Andrew Cecil Bennett was the new premier. His platform called for industrial development of the province. Building highways had not been a priority for the old government, but the Socreds knew that a network of good highways was needed to translate their development dreams into reality. The biggest projects Bennett envisioned were hydroelectric dams to provide cheap electricity to British Columbians and for export. Among these projects were the Mica and Arrow dams on the Columbia River, followed by the Bennett Dam on the Peace River.

Bennett appointed a Pentecostal minister to be his Minister of Public Works, a portfolio later renamed Ministry of Highways. The new minister was Phillip Arthur Gaglardi, the member for the riding of Kamloops. Gaglardi, the son of Italian immigrants, was the man for the job. He was flamboyant, had unbounded enthusiasm, and was willing to take chances. He was ready to show the world what he could do. But he was a political novice and relied strongly on the advice of his senior civil servants who had virtually run the province for as long as anyone cared to remember. They were not about to give up their little fiefdoms to a neophyte, but Gaglardi had his own ideas.

He announced that a network of new roads was going to cover the province and that his ministry was ready to do business with all comers as long as they could perform and do what was asked of them. This was what Ben Ginter had been waiting for. He was not interested in politics; he wanted to build roads. He was smart enough to know that it was the politicians who controlled the purse strings of the really big projects. Ben, by now, saw himself as an entrepreneur who could do anything, given half a chance. He was willing to take his chances with the new government. Ginter went to Victoria and tried to find out how he would get government contracts, but he was stonewalled.

Road construction in British Columbia was the domain of five established companies which guarded their position jealously. They saw nothing wrong in exchanging information on bidding among themselves and then deciding which project would be handled by whom. It was a closed shop. The chief engineer in Victoria told Ginter to go home since there was no chance for him to get a contract. Civil servants guarded the status quo against all outsiders who might upset it.

Ginter would later recall that while he was politely listening to the engineer and was properly deferential, he was boiling mad inside. He did not take his ire out on the engineer, whom he regarded as nothing but a paid flunky. He thought of other ways to join the lucrative highways business. He knew he could do any road job and could do it cheaper than any member of the existing cartel.

Ginter returned to Prince George after being told he didn't

belong. Then he made one of the smartest moves of his life. He went to see Ray Williston, the Socred Member of the Legislative Assembly for Fort George which included the city of Prince George. Williston, a former high school teacher and school superintendent in Prince George, had been elected in 1952 and later joined the cabinet as Minister of Lands, Forests and Water Resources. When Ginter contacted him, however, he was not yet a member of the cabinet. Williston sympathized with Ginter and promised to speak to Gaglardi for him. Ginter showed Williston bids that had been turned down by Victoria but were lower than the ones which the department had accepted.

Williston arranged a meeting between Ginter and Gaglardi. It should rank among those history-changing events that now and then occur. Gaglardi said he was curious to meet the man he had heard much about, and he was willing to be open-minded. "Ray Williston brought in this stocky fellow with a crew cut. He seemed really sure of himself and at once started to give me a speech. I lifted my hand to stop him and simply asked him if he could do the job should he get a contract. Ginter nodded enthusiastically and assured me he was more than ready to get started.

"I asked him about jobs he had done and asked him again if he could perform. Ginter assured me he could. So I told him I would tell the engineer to look at Ginter's tenders and that Ginter would hear from us," Gaglardi recalled some thirty years later.

One of Ginter's bids was below those of the old guard, and he got his first contract. It was the first time in British Columbia history that a minister had overruled the recommendations of the chief highway engineer. The contract called for the construction of a section of Highway 97 near the community of McLeese Lake, just north of Williams Lake in the Cariboo region of the province. Gaglardi must have had second thoughts about Ginter, because he went to the work site to inspect the project. "I could find no faults with his performance; in fact, he was doing an excellent job," said Gaglardi. "Over the years Ginter saved the taxpayers of British Columbia millions of dollars while doing an outstanding job," said the former highways minister.

Gaglardi took his wife along on this trip, and it was at McLeese Lake that Grace Ginter would meet both the minister and his wife Jenny for the first time. It was the start of a long friendship which would eventually make rumours fly. One contract led to the next and it did not take overly long before rumours had it that Ginter and Gaglardi were in cahoots. "He got the job done," Gaglardi said at the age of 80 in recalling the old days in an interview in his Kamloops office. He said Ginter was dependable and street-smart. "Oh, I knew rumours were flying but I can assure you I never received a dime from Ginter," Gaglardi said.

These rumours accused the highways minister of patronage where Ginter was concerned, and Ginter was rumoured to be making some money-losing deals only to cash in on major projects. Over the years Ginter constructed more than $300 million worth of roads throughout the province. Ginter was insulted by the rumours. He said it was easy enough to make money through hard work and business acumen. "When you tackle a project, everything has to be in place. Everything has to be just right when you want to do a good job, do it on time, and do it as it should be done. That will guarantee success," Ginter said.

Ray Williston recalls Ginter as a highly innovative operator with a natural instinct for publicity. Williston said he had many business dealings with Ginter in the years after their first meeting. "I always found him a good man to deal with. I respected Ginter and believe he respected me," Williston said, but he faulted Ginter for believing that he was an expert in every field simply because he had become an expert road builder.

My own involvement in the Ginter story began in 1964 when I came to Prince George after *The Vancouver Times*, a short-lived newspaper venture, folded. *The Prince George Citizen*, then under the editorship of Harry Boyle, former editor of *The Whitehorse Star* and later a judge of the British Columbia Supreme Court, was in the market for new reporters. Prince George was a journalistic backwater as far as reporters in the Lower Mainland were concerned.

However, I had enjoyed a stint with *The Kamloops Sentinel* before going to Vancouver after returning from Europe. There I had worked for the largest evening daily in Germany, *The Hamburger Abendblatt*. In fact, I returned to British Columbia because of a telephone call from Bill Forrest, one of the driving forces behind *The Vancouver Times*, requesting that I come back to Vancouver. But the start up for *The Times* had been postponed for a year, and I became a reporter at *The Sentinel* under the editorship of the able George Smith. He knew I had a job with *The Times* as soon as the paper started publication, but Smith did not mind my using his paper as a stopgap.

After a few months with *The Vancouver Times*, I became aware that the paper was not going to make it. Competing with *The Sun* and *The Province* was just not working. Staff were being laid off; but to the credit of management, it must be said, jobs were being secured for those they were forced to fire. When my turn came, I was asked if I wanted to go to Prince George.

Prince George? Where the hell was Prince George? After a wet all-night farewell, I was poured on the train, the Pacific Great Eastern Railway. At its terminus, I was told, lay Prince George. The temperature was about minus 20 Celsius, so I asked the conductor if the train was returning to Vancouver the same night. I was short of money, but would have washed dishes to escape this punishing cold.

No such luck. All I knew about Prince George was the name of the McDonald Hotel, and I imagined it was something like its namesake in Edmonton. Well, it wasn't. In fact, it was a noisy place where sleep would only come at a premium. On top of that, the change from the climate in Vancouver to the dry cold of the Interior caused me to come down with an extreme case of influenza.

Harry Boyle, whom I came to regard as one of the greatest human beings, made sure I was all right. He visited me daily while I was languishing in my hotel room. He said he knew I was ready to work when he asked me one day if there were anything else he could provide; and I told him, jokingly, I could use a case of beer. Harry frowned, but he brought the merchandise an hour later. Next day I was at work.

I was assigned to cover the labour beat. The hottest story in town was a disagreement between the International Union of Operating Engineers, Local 115, and Ben Ginter Construction Co. Ltd. I talked to union officials Derek Joergensen and Jack Whittacker, but to round out the story I called Ginter. I had been informed by *The Citizen's* former labour reporter that Ginter was almost never available and was very hard to talk to. Much to my surprise I was put through to him at once and the man talked to me.

However, he said, he would see me at his office, because he did not like giving interviews on the telephone. Ginter's compound was just around the corner from *The Citizen*. I was ushered in to see the big tycoon at once. Ben was grinning when we shook hands and he asked me to sit down. "Well, son, what do you want to know?" he asked.

I related the accusations the unions had made and asked him for a comment. He told me his side of the story, as I furiously took notes. Then he said I should call union headquarters in Prince George right away to check to see if he weren't telling the truth. I dialled the union's number and waited. Joergensen came to the phone, and I told him what Ben had said. Meanwhile, sitting across from Ginter who sat behind his big desk, I noticed that Ginter's hand had disappeared into his lap. Derek was not holding back when he answered the questions and used some rather colourful language in describing his adversary. Ginter just smiled and nodded. I had a story.

Two days later Joergenson called and asked me about the telephone call. He wanted to know from where I had made the call. I told him and he asked me to visit him at union headquarters. Once there, he showed me a transcript of the conversation between him and myself. I was totally taken aback: Ginter had taped the conversation. His hand had not been in his lap; it had been on a button under his desk. This button activated a tape recorder.

I was livid. My integrity had been impugned, and Ginter was going to pay for it. Never mind his being the construction baron, he had compromised me. How could I ever be an impartial observer the way newspaper reporters were supposed to be? I called Ginter, and to my surprise he agreed to see me at once. He smiled when I entered his office ready to tell him off.

"I know why you are here and what's bugging you," he said, rather disarmingly. "Hey, kid, don't take it so serious, we all got to learn the hard way. I admit, I took advantage of you and promise you it won't happen again. I did not expect you to come in here and raise shit. I thought you are just like the others: once I chewed them up, they stayed away," Ginter said. "I just wanted to see what you'd do."

Having been taught by my middle-class German parents to be polite and respectful to my elders, I told Ginter I was hurt by his machinations and that I would asked for a change of beats because I did not think I could ever trust him again.

I think Ginter felt bad about the situation, and he said if I would report straight forward, he would never pull any punches. He offered his hand on the deal and we shook. During the following years, Ginter never dodged any questions; and according to his executive assistant, Louise McCormick, he believed I would report stories straight. We had established perimeters and developed mutual respect. Over the next ten years or so I never had grounds to believe that Ben Ginter was not straight with me. He was a reliable source.

Ginter freely admitted he made a lot of money from government contracts, but insisted it always was honest money. While this was true and confirmed by several of Ginter's former executives,

Ginter used a different way to gain influence. His stock-in-trade was favours. He would send an excavator out to someone who needed earth work done. He would send a painting crew to someone else if a building needed a new coat of paint, and he would do numerous favours for others as "markers." When the time came when he needed some assistance, he would call in these "markers" and have the favours returned. But he never engaged in cash bribery or dishonest cash dealings.

Ginter's first successful bid opened the door for others. Gaglardi recalled that soon after Ginter's first job for his department, about twenty-six other companies began to submit bids, effectively breaking the cartel. Gaglardi opened the bidding to anyone who could perform, but still insisted that contractors be bondable, and be Canadian or at least have a Canadian partner to work on government jobs. The highways department often called on Ginter when it needed no-bid jobs done by day labour, as Ginter's crews were always ready.

"Ginter and Gaglardi" or in Kamloops "Gaglardi and Ginter," became a common byword in British Columbia and since Phil Gaglardi was also a minister of the gospel the slogan was enlarged to "Ginter, Gaglardi and God," a sort of triumvirate lording it over the province. It was not even then meant as a compliment.

Years later Gaglardi would laugh about it. "I must admit it was a catchy slogan, but I tell you again in all honesty there never was even one shady deal between me and Ben Ginter. Everything was on the up and up. We did business because it was good business. Good for Ginter, good for the minister and, most of all, good for the taxpayers. The province profited greatly from Ginter's efficiency."

B.C. Attorney-General Robert Bonner, centre, visits a Ginter
Construction project, one of many throughout the province.

One of the many rumours said that Ginter and Gaglardi's wives were related; some even said the women were sisters. "Nothing could be farther from the truth. They came from very different backgrounds and the Ginters and Gaglardis were not related, but they became friends over the years," said Phil Gaglardi.

Ginter had become part of the tremendous industrial boom British Columbia experienced during the 1950s and 1960s. The northern part of the province became a key area in this development. Multi-million dollar pulp mills sprang up almost everywhere, and huge hydroelectric projects, such as the Bennett Dam at Hudson's Hope, were built with Ginter part of it all.

Ginter watched with interest a scheme that was to become known as the Wenner- Gren project. This called for, among other things, the building of a monorail through the Rocky Mountain Trench to facilitate speedier industrial development in mining and hydroelectric power. Axel Wenner-Gren was a Swedish multimillionaire who made his money during the war. That became his downfall in British Columbia. When it became known he had dealt not only with the Allies, but also with the Axis Powers during hostilities, public opinion turned against him. Premier Bennett, always sensitive to the mood of the voters, cancelled the project. Ginter regretted the cancellation in private because the project would have provided numerous jobs for his companies. Publicly he agreed that Wenner-Gren, because of his wartime activities, was not the right person to help develop British Columbia.

Ginter cleared the sites for the pulp mills in Prince George and Prince Rupert. He paved Highway 16 east and west of Prince George. He opened the road link between Prince George and McBride and, with it, Prince George's link to the rest of Canada

Ben Ginter, centre, makes a flying visit to a highway project where he consults with on-site engineers.

to the east. Anywhere motorists drove in mainland British Columbia, they could be sure they were driving on pavement laid down by Ginter Construction. At Quesnel, Ginter built the Quesnel River bridge and the overpass. The steel for this bridge came all the way from West Germany. When he checked on his order, Ginter took his wife along on a trip to Europe wanting her to know his European roots.

His energy and enthusiasm as a construction boss passed ordinary imagination. In Prince George, he was involved in building the expansion of the runways at the city's airport and he built the five-hundred-mile stretch of the Yellowhead Highway to the Alberta border. Most of it was constructed in adverse conditions through difficult territory. Ginter built the Stewart-Cassiar

Erecting the foundation of yet another bridge by Ginter Construction.

Highway in northwest British Columbia and his crews were forced to construct a 1,200 mile detour to get to Burrage Creek. Equipment had to be shipped north and west up the Alaska Highway, then shipped down south again to the work site. During the winter, crews built ice bridges, laying down gravel and trees on the ice surface and backing the materials up with snow. They then re-laid trees and gravel again. It was backbreaking work, but the crews worked around the clock until it was done. Ginter set construction records. He moved more than 500,000

Tons of concrete were poured in the expansion of B.C.'s highway system. Ben's crews poured much of it.

Ginter crews pour asphalt at the extended runway of the Prince George airport in the 1960s.

tons of dirt in one season and built eighteen miles of road during the short construction season in the province's North.

A Prince George man found out that dealing with Ginter was not what his past experience had prepared him for. He signed a contract to ship the bunkhouses for the Stewart-Cassiar job, using the route Ginter had used. There were problems with breakdowns the subcontractor had to repair along the way. He believed Ginter should pay for all the delays. Ginter believed otherwise. He said he had given the man a contract to deliver the bunkhouses at a certain price and that price was all he was going to get. Ginter agreed to pay for some of the repairs because he could see they were caused by the hard terrain. Otherwise, he insisted on the agreed-upon price and that was the end of the discussion.

It was one of Ginter's peculiarities that he would lay his cards on the table and make a deal up front. Once it was concluded, he would not budge, and he would certainly not pay extras. If the person he dealt with ran into unexpected problems, Ginter would shrug and say it was the man's own fault. He should have calculated every possible risk and have included it in his price.

4

T HE BOOM DID NOT PASS the City of Prince George by. Houses were rented or sold as soon as they were put up. Hotels rarely had a vacancy. The city was growing. Streets were being paved and new areas were absorbed into the city. Ginter did his share of paving. Yet, he was an outcast in his chosen city in much the same way as Prince George has never been fully recognized by the rest of the province, especially by Vancouver and the Lower Mainland. The idea that Prince George was a good place to come from, not to live in, was and — still is — a common attitude in the southern part of the province. The provincial news media, represented mainly by Vancouver's two daily newspapers, rarely printed news from Prince George unless it was sensational and showed the "unsophisticated way of life up North."

The late Aaron Thompson, city manager of Prince George at the time of Ginter's ascent to importance, often related a story of a Vancouver reporter, who later became a national columnist, is still working as such, and so will remain unnamed. This reporter arrived in Prince George and promptly hit the bars. He talked to people while drinking, but took no notes. The police guided him back to his hotel, because he could not find his own way. The following day, suffering from a big hangover, he returned to Vancouver and wrote a story.

"That yarn was almost a total fabrication, and it was full of statements about booze, prostitutes, street fights, and rowdy behaviour," Thompson said. Officials in Prince George were embarrassed and checked the reporter's statements by visiting the same places he had spent the night. It turned out there was not even one fight; there had been no rowdiness. In fact, it had been one of the quietest of nights, according to police records. Thompson vowed he would run this particular reporter out of town on the rail, should he ever show his face in town again. To the best of everyone's knowledge, the man has never come back.

It was not the only time a reporter from the Lower Mainland tried to write about Prince George after a few superficial interviews and spending considerable time at one watering hole or another. Journalists were easily seduced by the city's reputation, and they did their best to enhance this reputation. The late Vancouver Sun columnist Jack Wassermann came to Prince George to interview Ben Ginter who entertained him at his "mansion on the hill," as Wassermann called it in his column. Later Ben drove Wassermann to his downtown hotel. A few days later Wassermann recounted his adventures in Prince George in the Vancouver Sun. He complained he had been unable to sleep because of the loud music being played all night somewhere near his hotel. He called Prince George the "capital of all-night partying." Local reporters checked out Wassermann's story, but were unable to find out where this loud music had come from. Finally, the explanation came from the hotel manager. Each room of the hotel had a radio set in the night stand next to the bed and canned music was piped in around the clock. It took a special switch to turn the music off, which the columnist, after being fêted by Ginter, was unable to find.

Wassermann did not write much about his Ginter interview on this occasion, being more fascinated by this mysterious party music and finding the situation disgraceful. This attitude of the news media has lasted to this day. While the newspapers seem to have learned that the "Northern Capital," as Prince George calls itself today, is a progressive modern place to live, television coverage of Prince George is still sadly inadequate.

When the internationally-known Prince George children's choir Die Meistersingers won a major trophy in Austria in 1989, BCTV sent a camera crew and one of its better known reporters. The story appeared as part of a newscast and opened with a view of smoke belching from the stacks of the pulp mills, followed by logs being cut by giant saws. The reporter, her hair and make-up in perfect condition, opened her oral coverage with something about a small town nestled at the "edge of the wilderness" as she briefly mentioned the achievements of the choir after speaking at length about the "city at the edge of the wilderness."

More recently, provincial television snubbed Prince George over the the convocation of the new University of Northern British Columbia. A BCTV official told a city councillor that BCTV would cover Prince George should a Boeing 747 jumbo jet crash there, but only then. This example shows that news coverage of Prince George by provincial television has not changed much from Ginter's days.

Ben Ginter was never popular in Prince George. When he arrived, he was a nobody. Those who deemed themselves to be the city's elite ignored him. With the growth of his fortune, however, he could no longer be ignored. Ginter became a member of the local Kiwanis Club, the chamber of commerce, the golf and curling club, the fall fair society and the Masonic Lodge. The boy from Minitonas had entered Prince George society. Or so he thought.

The people who set the tone in Prince George were those whose parents had arrived when the city was incorporated in 1915 or in 1914 when the Grand Trunk Pacific Railway arrived. These were the people after whom streets were named and who were busy in civic affairs. Ginter had no time for this kind of activity and the elite resented his attitude. While others may have had "comfortable" incomes, Ginter was still working to get "comfortable." He felt those with money called themselves "comfortable" because to call themselves rich would be rude.

Ben Ginter had only himself to blame for his lack of acceptance in Prince George, and, for that matter, in the many other places where he did business. Ben Ginter did not like paying bills and delayed payments for as long as possible. He simply ignored small debts and anyone reminding him that he was owed money would often get Ben's standard answer: "Sue me."

One of his favourite ploys was to ignore a bill. If a creditor wrote Ben's firms after submitting a bill, Ginter would not respond, and telephone enquiries were useless. However, if the same creditor came down to Ginter's corporate headquarters to ask for payment, Ginter would appear to be shocked that the bill was still outstanding. He would tell his accountants to pay the bill at once and chastize the accounting staff openly. Then he would apologize to the man he had stiffed, portraying himself as totally innocent. The man would take his payment and go straight to the bank, happy that he had received money from Ginter. The accountants, however, were furious with Ginter because he had told them to hold the bill until the last possible minute, but now they were the culprits. One accountant said he still does not believe Ginter withheld payment deliberately. He said the construction company dealt on a 90-day payment basis which was needed because it took that long to process the paperwork.

An example of strictly sticking to the letter of the deal, regardless of how it may have affected others, was Ginter's treatment of a local automobile dealer. Ginter was looking for a fleet of pick-up trucks for his construction business. He needed several dozen vehicles and the local dealer made him a good offer. Of course, a dealer in a town the size of Prince George was unable to handle the after-sale service without having to expand his facilities.

Ginter accepted the deal and the company brought in the trucks. Warranties in those days seldom exceeded one year, and the dealer had built new service bays for the days when he would continue to service Ginter's fleet after the warranties had expired. Once the trucks had been delivered, Ginter made good use of the service warranties. It was a great deal for Ben. He got his pick-ups serviced free as the contract specified, and he had received a good deal on the vehicles because of the large number he bought.

When the warranties expired, Ginter serviced the vehicles in his own shop. The car dealer faced bankruptcy. When he approached Ginter, he was informed that it was not in Ginter's interests to have the car dealer service the trucks. The dealership went into receivership and was sold. This was just one of many similar Ginter deals. He would pick up the telephone and place orders with local firms. No purchase orders or other accounting procedures were mentioned. He would not mention his orders to his accounting staff who would then question the invoice when it arrived. At first local businessmen were quite happy to do business with the big outfit, but they soon learned Ginter would not pay bills unless there was a purchase order to go with them. When he made the purchases, he never bothered to get an order; hence the bill would not be paid.

Prince George businessmen were nonplused by this attitude and practice until they saw the reasoning behind Ginter's methods: how else could anyone make so much money and become a millionaire unless he cut every corner he possibly could? One way was by not paying small bills when they were due, and Ginter had no qualms about any of his methods. If those businessmen were stupid enough to take an order without a purchase order number, they deserved what they got.

It was not a way to make friends, however. Business dealings with Ginter were not welcomed. On the other hand, the same businessmen fawned when Ginter looked at them personally or favoured them with his attention. After all, he was a big, important man.

Ginter could also be very charitable. He would contribute gladly when approached by churches, sports teams, service clubs, or anyone else. This, however, was not done simply from altruism. A sports team, for instance, that carried Ginter's sponsorship was expected to win in its league, whatever it was. If it did not come out on top one season, the team had better look for another sponsor.

Ben Ginter would also help others if they wanted to get ahead in business, as he recognized a sound proposal. The dealership of a diesel engine repair shop was for sale in Prince George and three employees wanted to buy it, but were short of money. Through an intermediary, they made a proposal to Ginter to lend the money, which Ben did. He had checked with his own diesel shop foreman who vouched for the good work the three men did. Then he lent the full sum to purchase the dealership outright. He demanded only that they issue post-dated cheques for the repayment and pay double the prime-rate. It was a satisfactory arrangement for everybody and the shop is still doing business in Prince George today.

One place Ben Ginter liked to visit was the Vienna Schnitzelhaus, a German restaurant operated by Hans Rosenlehner. The two men got along well. Ginter had helped Rosenlehner financially when he opened the restaurant which became immensely popular under Rosenlehner's stewardship. Rosenlehner, in turn, immortalized Ginter by having his patron's face painted on the huge fireplace along with a few other faces. Ginter was rather pleased about that and never failed to point to the painting when he entertained at the Vienna. Ginter would drop in, sit at the bar, and talk to the regulars. He would buy a round, always expecting to have another bought for him. Hans Rosenlehner was one of the few Prince George businessmen who attended Ginter's funeral service in Vancouver. A few years later the restaurateur died in a plane crash in the Interior.

Anyone doing business with Ginter had to be on constant alert. He owned what he called his "airline," a collection of a few planes, including a Grumman Widgeon, an Aero Commander, and a deHavilland single-engined Otter. He rented space at the airport

44

in Prince George and eventually set up a hangar. Ginter planned to apply for a federal licence to fly freight and charters in northern British Columbia. He grandly called this company Imperial Airways Limited.

Hearing of his plans, two men from the Lower Mainland — Ginter's executives called them carpetbaggers — came to see Ginter. They wanted to sell prefabricated metal buildings which he could use for many purposes including hangars at the airport. Their asking price was $135,000. Ginter was interested, but did not like the price. They negotiated and Ginter managed to reduce the price to $70,000 for all the components to be delivered to Prince George. The carpetbaggers were short on cash and agreed that Ginter could deduct the freight charges from the purchase price. Ginter paid them $35,000 up front.

The buildings were delivered, but Ginter refused to pay more than he already had, saying the men had misrepresented the facts about the buildings. Ginter had turned over the blue-prints to his engineers, who found that, while the roof would be able to carry a snow load of 65 pounds per square foot, the uprights would be unable to support the roof with this kind of a snow load. He threatened to sue to have his money returned unless the two men were willing to accept what they already had received as a final payment. The carpetbaggers decided it was better to have $35,000 in their pockets than a law suit around their necks. They disappeared. Ginter's crews erected the hangar and simply doubled up on the upright supports to ensure a safe building. It was easy and done without additional cost because of the large number of spare parts included in the deal. The hangar is still in use today.

Ben Ginter never got a licence for the operation of an airline, but he used his planes extensively. He bought the single-engine Otter in the United States, and he thought he was getting a bargain. As it turned out, in his haste to get the plane, he out-smarted himself. The purchase price was $30,000. This was too good for Ginter to pass up. There was a big drawback, however. The Otter had seen service with the United Nations in the Congo. The plane had been built in Canada for export and, therefore, lacked some of the safety features required in Canada but not abroad. The cost of bringing it up to Canadian standard was prohibitive and Ginter got rid of the plane as soon as he could. It was a mistake buying the aircraft without checking it out, Ginter said. He explained he did not have much experience with planes. After the Otter fiasco, he would not make the same mistake again.

He preferred to be flown in the Grumman Widgeon, a float plane. Since there are more lakes than airstrips in British Columbia, it made good sense to own a float plane. Ginter used it for fishing trips and family outings as well as for business. But even here he looked for the cheapest way of operating. He hired a pilot for the Widgeon for the season from April to October. The pay he offered was not top dollar, since this was one of the few jobs for which Ginter did not have to pay union wages. He promised the pilot that, if he served the full season, Ginter would pay him a good-sized bonus. Ginter then laid off the pilot two weeks before the season was completed, saying weather conditions made it impossible to fly anymore that year. He no longer required the pilot. He did not pay the bonus.

One man, at least, got the best of Ginter. In fact, it is safe to say he cheated Ginter. This man owned a hotel in the British Columbia

Family fishing using the company Grumman Widgeon. Ben, left, with son James, pilot, and two employees at a northern B.C. lake.

Interior, and Ginter was trying to get him to take Tartan draught beer in his beer parlour. According to prevailing liquor control board rules, hotel operators could apply for changes in the type of draught beer served, but had to wait six months before the actual change could take place. The hotel man applied for Tartan draught after Ginter had guaranteed a loan of $75,000. As soon as the loan had been secured, the owner applied for a change in beer and after six months switched again to another brand. There was nothing Ginter could do, except to complain bitterly about how he had been cheated in the "dirtiest industry in Canada."

Ginter, like many other self-made men, always had to be first in everything he undertook. In his companies, there was never any doubt as to who was in charge. Ginter reserved final decisions on just about everything for himself. When he had made up his mind he would follow his own counsel, regardless of advice from others. This created much confusion and hurt feelings with his executives. Ginter blithely chose to overlook this executive anxiety. It was his money and his business. They were his employees. He would do whatever he deemed to be right. Anyone objecting to his decisions could find another job. Those who voiced their doubts about any Ginter decision could find themselves fired on the spot. Employees at the Prince George brewery said they were always aware when Ginter was on the premises. The mood would be sombre, if not depressed. They never knew what faults the boss might find and what he would do. It was best to keep quiet and do one's work while the man was present. Ginter was an exacting, unpredictable boss.

Not all who worked for Ginter felt that way. Some of his former staff at head office said that he was the best boss they ever had and that he was always polite and courteous to them. They had no complaints and did not feel intimidated by his presence. They always knew whether Ginter was present or not by where his black Thunderbird was parked. If he was at the office, the T-Bird was sitting right in front of the door. If he was absent, it was parked by a fence.

Ginter was fond of that car, and he would always drive it at high speeds. Travelling from Prince George to Houston, some 336 kilometres away, he often completed the trip in about two hours. Considering the state of the road, it was quite an accomplishment, also totally illegal. On one occasion, when returning from Houston, he had brake trouble. By the time he came to Burns Lake, still some 224 kilometres from Prince George, all brake fluid was lost, but the problem could not be repaired at Burns Lake. Ginter decided to drive on. He averaged more than 160 kilometres per hour without brakes. Ginter liked taking chances.

5

A TYPICAL INCIDENT OF EMPLOYER-employee relations, Ginter-style, took place in the summer of 1967. Ginter had acquired controlling interest in *The Prince George Progress*, a weekly newspaper which had been founded by Robert E. Strom, a former advertising salesman for the local daily, *The Prince George Citizen*. *The Progress* had done quite well in the early years, but it had not done so well lately. Ginter, by now quite autocratic and ruthless, felt he needed a newspaper to express his unedited views. Ginter was not alone, as it seemed to be a fad during the 1960s for rich people to own their own newspapers.

Ginter had become disenchanted with the way most journalists treated him, even though he never missed a chance to talk to them. But he did not trust them to put his views across the way he meant them to come across. What better way to correct this problem than to have his own newspaper and control the journalists who worked for it? He was also genuinely interested in helping Strom, as he had known the young publisher for many years. Once Ginter bought *The Progress*, Strom stayed on as publisher in charge of operations; however, Ginter took great interest in what would be published in his paper.

Strom was a native of Prince George, and his parents A.W. and Laura Strom were well-known. Strom grew up knowing Ginter since he was in the same social circle as Strom's parents. When a teenager, Strom had always been aware of Ginter because the man was gaining prominence and reputation. Robert Strom, nick-named "Bobbie," took a job with *The Prince George Citizen* and worked in advertising sales. When he turned twenty-one, he started his own newspaper, the weekly *Prince George Progress*. For four years he managed to publish, but then ran into some financial problems and turned to Ginter who became a fifty-fifty partner with him. Besides the weekly newspaper, they produced a monthly magazine called *Industrial Progress*. It grandiosely claimed to reach as far as the Yukon and the Northwest Territories and dealt mainly with issues concerning the North.

"Ben could be impossible at times, but there was another side to him. He could be incredibly generous and thoughtful, but most people never got to see this side," Strom said in retrospect. He also pointed out that Ginter interfered much less than was commonly believed, while they had had many arguments about what should or should not be published. Strom liked Ginter, but objected to Ben's habit of calling at any hour just to talk or to ask Bob to go for a ride with him and then talk in the car.

Mel Rothenburger, now editor of *The Daily News* in Kamloops and the author of a biography of Phil Gaglardi, the former highways minister, was the *Progress* editor during the 1967 Williams Lake Stampede. Stampedes and similar small-town events usually had beer gardens and Ginter promoted his prod-ucts heavily at such happenings. Rothenburger assigned photog-rapher Lew Armstrong to go to Williams Lake to take some pictures. When he returned, Rothenburger decided to publish a picture page and among the photos he used was one which showed a drunken reveller carrying a box of beer under his arm.

Rothenburger picks up the story:

"I remember this day of infamy as though it was yesterday. I was sitting at my desk in the office of *The Prince George Progress* which was located on the second floor of a former warehouse. It was in June 1967. The telephone rang, and it was Ginter on the other end in his typically snarly mood. I was about to find out just how snarly he could be.

'Who took those pictures of the Williams Lake Stampede?' he asked me.

'Lew Armstrong,' I told him, referring to our staff photographer.

'Who put them in the paper?'

'Well, Peter Vander Leelie dummied them,' I said, my curiosity beginning to rise. Peter, a bright young kid barely out of high school, was our layout editor.

'I want them both fired,' Ginter announced, 'I won't have pictures of my competitors in my newspaper.' Suddenly it all became clear. One of the pictures in Lew's photo feature was of a stampede celebrant carrying a box of Carling Pilsner. The label was visible in less than a square inch of space. I was momentarily stunned, but without thinking twice, I puffed out my chest and told Ginter, 'Well, if you are going to fire them, you better fire me too. I am responsible for everything that goes into the paper.' I knew Ginter reasonably well and

I knew he would not fire two key staff members over such a silly thing if it meant losing the editor, too.

'Okay,' Ginter said without a second's hesitation, 'you're fired, too.' That was that and he would not back down. He followed it up with comments to *The Prince George Citizen* about there being far too many people employed by *The Progress* anyway, failing to endear himself to the rest of the staff. Lew, Peter and I held autographing sessions in which we signed copies of the offending photo. They were quite popular. I still have one hanging in my office today.

My wife and I packed our belongings into a Budget Rent-A-Trailer and prepared to head south with our newborn baby to look for new employment. The day I walked out of *The Progress* for the last time I said to publisher Bob Strom he had not backed me up.

Bob said, 'I tried, Mel,' but I knew he could not stand up to Ginter."

Peter Vander Leelie, who now also works for *The Kamloops Daily News*, recalled his firing well. Rothenburger informed him that, over the telephone, Ginter had just fired the three people responsible for taking and publishing the picture with the offending label. Rothenberger, unlike Ginter, at least passed on the news in face-to-face meetings. Vander Leelie also packed up and left Prince George, but was asked to return a few weeks later to work for *The Prince George North Star*. This turned out to be the successor to *The Progress*, and Ginter's entry into the world of daily newspapers.

He had just decided to go daily overnight. As editor he hired Rollie Rose, a well-known newspaperman from Vancouver Island. The paper claimed it was employee-owned, and Ginter's name did not appear anywhere. On its editorial masthead the paper proclaimed rather pretentiously: Responsibility, Justice, Truth and Compassion.

It was a short-lived venture because the paper failed to attract major advertisers, such as food store chains and car dealers. Ginter tried to use his considerable influence by going directly to head offices of some of the food chains and car manufacturers, only to be told that it was up to local management to decide to advertise with *The North Star*. Despite desperate attempts to make its advertising attractive to these retailers, the paper was not to be. In the final edition on June 30, 1970, the front page carried a self-pitying but self-congratulatory not-very-original story. Just about every newspaper that ever ceased publication has used the same line.

The story went:

North Star succumbs to economic pressure

"*The North Star* has ceased publication with today's edition. Owner-employees say they have run out of money, and with no promise of support from the business community, and tight economic development, they are unable to continue to publish one of Canada's few competitive newspapers.

"We have made the decision to discontinue publication with regret, but we have no alternative. There has been almost no trend established within the last eight weeks, certainly not enough to warrant further financial support from Mr. Ben Ginter. In fact, we do not consider it realistic to request consideration of more support by Mr. Ginter, in view of what has happened. *The North Star* began publication on May 2, amid national speculation whether it could survive. A young fighting staff was put together and backed by industrialist Ben Ginter, who believed in the people and the need of a second daily newspaper in the North. *The North Star* set out to do what the experts said could not be done.

"After four weeks of publication the newspaper appealed to the business community for support and for ten days its life blood — advertising — increased, but not enough to pull it out of the woods, but sufficiently enough to believe a trend was being formed. But during the ensuing two weeks, with a tighter-than-ever economy descending upon Prince George, advertising revenue dropped off again, until Monday when *The North Star* published only eight pages.

Two things led to the death of *The North Star.* It never did enjoy the majority support of the business community, even though larger commerce like Woodward's, Hudson's Bay and Stedman's appeared to grasp the usefulness of two daily newspapers in a growing community and a restrictive economy. Perhaps it was the latter that led to non-support, we don't know, perhaps it was simply bad timing.

We do not hang our heads in shame at failing. We gave it a good try and won a lot of friends along the way, especially with the working man. He liked *The North Star* and told us so. But we were never allowed to develop the newspaper the way we wanted to. To do this you have to be on solid financial footing.

"Though *The North Star* disappears today, we have left a legacy of a better newspaper standard in Prince George. *The Citizen* has become a better newspaper because of us and you, as a reader, can demand that it will not be allowed to slide back to its old ways. *The North Star* will now turn to the weekly field. We hope Prince George will support us in our new role because we feel there is a place in this young community for us. We intend to keep our plant intact and will again be prepared to look at the daily field if and when the economy becomes better and if you demonstrate a real need for a second daily.

"Staff and management express gratitude to those people who did support us and especially Mr. Ginter who was a tower of strength during our fight, for without him there would have been no *North Star*. We feel it is better to have tried and failed than never to have tried at all."

Peter Vander Leelie remembered: "It was late in the summer when Ginter appeared in the newsroom flanked by what I would call accountant types. They only stayed a few minutes and then left. He had not spoken to the staff. About 11:30 in the morning, with a mind full of rumours but no announcements, I picked up a copy of *The North Star*. It was the last edition, obviously. It had a big numerals screen overprinted on the front page: 30. I never touched a drop of Ginter's beer after that." The printing of the number 30 at the end of a news story signals to an editor that the story is complete and no other additions are expected. It meant the same when *The North Star* carried a large 30 on its front page. There would not be another edition and Ben Ginter was out of the newspaper business. Weekly publication was never resumed.

After Ginter had fired Rothenburger and Vander Leelie and Armstrong, he called me and offered me the editor's job. I had a good job with *The Citizen* and did not really want to work for a weekly newspaper. I thanked Ginter and declined. I still feel it was the right decision, something which was brought home to me several years later. I was then working for *The Edmonton Journal* and Ginter called one evening to ask me dine with him at the Chateau Lacombe in Edmonton. After we finished our meal, Ginter asked me to come up to his suite for a drink. He opened the door, and there was another man inside the entrance.

"Mr. Wenzel, this is Karl. Karl, this is Mr. Wenzel," Ginter said, making the introductions.

"Karl, get Mr. Wenzel a drink," Ginter ordered, "and the usual for me." Karl complied and withdrew to the other end of the room, taking no part in our conversation.

"Karl, refill Mr. Wenzel's drink," Ginter said in a rather brusque tone of voice. When Karl came with the drink, while Ginter used the bathroom, I asked Karl if he was Ginter's manservant.

He looked at me and said, "No, Mr. Wenzel, I am not Mr. Ginter's personal servant, I am the general manager of his Red Deer brewery." Suddenly I recalled the job offer and my refusal and I was glad because I was certain I could not have tolerated being treated like that. I would not have lasted long in Ginter's employ.

6

WITH HIS INCREASING SUCCESS, Ben grew expansive and felt he could pass judgment on anything and everything. According to Phil Gaglardi, Ben Ginter had become greedy. "When he bought the brewery I called him and told him that, as a born-again Baptist, he should not get involved with alcohol in any form. He just laughed and said his connection with alcohol was only to provide employment for others. Ben had become greedy and there was no way of stopping him," Gaglardi said.

Of course, this was at a time when the alliance between him and Ginter had fallen apart because road construction had slowed considerably. Also Ginter was no longer as much dependent on Gaglardi as he had been in the beginning. Ginter had made some negative remarks about his mentor saying the minister was getting too complacent in his job, and it was time for a change. Oddly, Gaglardi did not explain why he called Ginter a born-again Baptist, since Ben was not much of a church-going man.

Others who were close to Ginter in his heydays said buying and operating a brewery was his biggest mistake. They believe Ginter should have stayed with the construction business. Even owning the Prince George brewery was not too bad, in their opinion, but the attempt to build the empire Ginter envisioned rivalling that of Molson's was bound to fail. Ginter just did not have the resources. He should have been satisfied with his achievements as a construction millionaire and regional brewer. This horizon, however, was too small for his ambitions. Some people, including former Ginter executives, believe to this day that Ginter felt he would be more socially acceptable as a beer baron than as a construction tycoon. After all, there were quite a few construction tycoons, but how many beer barons were there in Canada?

While many of Ginter's regular employees found him to be a good boss and his firms good places to work, the executives didn't find it so easy. They would get high-sounding titles which usually meant nothing. Ginter would assign a project to one of his highly qualified people and let him work on it for some time. When the plan was completed, Ginter would often overrule his expert's conclusions and apply his own solutions. This was not exactly morale boosting for the manager or executive. Ginter's top personnel often would not know who was responsible for what. He would make cross-assignments and different projects would often overlap areas of responsibility. Joe Rinaldi, who acted as Ginter's legal advisor for eight years, said Ginter would have achieved many of his goals if he had let his executives work on their own. Ginter had top men in every field working for him, but interfered often or re-did the job himself in his own way. When Ginter called, his men had to be ready. It did not matter where they were, what they were doing or what time it was. Rinaldi said he was called out of class at the University of British Columbia and told to fly to Winnipeg. When he told Ginter he was working on his finals, Ginter replied he could do that next semester and he expected him to be on his way on the next available flight. "When Ginter told you he wanted you on a job, you had better be prepared to do it at once or start to look around for another job."

Hank Binder, the fellow Minitonian, said he quit Ginter's employ several times, but always went back when called. At one time, as reward and enticement, Ginter offered him a partnership in a trailer court in Prince George on the basis of eighty per cent of profit for Ginter and twenty per cent for Binder. When Binder objected to the lopsided partnership, Ginter offered to let him keep the corner grocery store profits at the park — which were meagre at best. Binder also was called on to do numerous other jobs. He would run the brewery, and, when he quit, Ginter called him back. Some time later Ginter offered to buy a hotel in Phoenix, Arizona, for Binder as a retirement project. But when they found a suitable hotel, Ginter suggested one of his sisters would help Binder manage the place.

However, Binder had finally learned to decline. He knew management would not be in his hands, but in those of Ginter's sister. Binder still believes Ginter never cared for anyone else but himself. All deals were subject to Ginter changing his mind and leaving others out in the cold. Still, Binder would always go back when Ginter wanted him, much to the disgust of Binder's wife. She said the years her husband worked for Ginter were the hardest of their lives. She recalled that several holidays the Binders planned had to be cancelled because Ginter found a job for her husband which had to be carried out without delay. "Once we had to give up a trip to a family meeting because Ben wanted Hank to do something else," Mrs. Binder said.

When Ginter was at the apex of his career he was in charge not only of the construction business, concentrated in British Columbia, but also of seven brewing operations throughout western Canada. He was involved with a multi-million dollar pulp mill with international ties. In a more civic-minded vein, he tried to revive the fall fair in Prince George. He put all his energies into all of his ventures. He also believed that to be forewarned was to be forearmed. He said it never hurt to know what the opposition was up to; he applied his own intelligence methods.

One way of getting information and other negotiating tidbits was to get his opponents drunk. One Thanksgiving weekend he invited officials of one of the unions with which he had problems to his office. He told them he was willing to sign a contract. The men arrived, read the contract, and everyone affixed his name to the document. There were handshakes all around and Ginter called for drinks. It was an occasion for celebration, he said.

And celebrate they did, not noticing that Ginter was not drinking as much as they were. Ben kept on filling the glasses, and the union officials kept drinking. When the celebration ended in the early morning hours, everyone went home. When the union officials arrived at their office Tuesday, they were in for a shock. The copy of the contract was not the contract they had signed, although their signatures were at the bottom. While they had been drinking Ginter had the contract spirited away and one page was substituted for another which had deleted facts both parties had agreed to but Ginter had not liked. The union was furious and any trust they may have had in Ginter was lost. The story got around and unions became extremely vigilant in future dealings with Ben Ginter.

A similar incident took place when Ginter wanted to find out

what a pair of Federal Bureau of Investigations (FBI) agents from
Washington D.C. were going to say in a report about a claim Ginter
had made against the United States government. Ginter had bid
on a construction project in Alaska and won the contract. He
shipped equipment to that state only to find out that American
unions strongly objected to a Canadian contractor on a government job. Ben had to ship the machinery back to Canada at
considerable cost to himself. He billed the federal government in
Washington for his costs. Through connections in Washington,
Ginter managed to have his claim accepted, but the United States
government wanted to check Ginter's books for the correctness
of his claim. Two FBI agents, both accountants, were sent to Prince
George. They worked for several days and resisted all invitations
to Ginter's big house after a day's work. However, Ginter persuaded them to accept his invitation once they had completed
their job. Ginter wanted to apply his tried and true method of
pumping the men full of booze, hoping they would talk about
what they found and what their recommendation for payment
might be. One of the agents did not mind getting drunk, but the
other would not touch a drop.

Neither man wanted to talk about his findings. When Ginter
realized there was no way to get the agents to talk he told his legal
adviser Joe Rinaldi to take them back to their downtown hotel.
Joe lost control of the car coming down the hill from the Ginter
estate and landed in a snowbank. No one was injured, but when
he tried to get the car free he hit a stump and twisted an axle on the
vehicle. Ginter had noticed their predicament and after a while
went to help. By this time it was so cold that even the second FBI
man did not turn down the offer of a drink from a bottle which

Ginter just happened to have in his pocket. The Americans never divulged their findings or what recommendations they were going to make to Washington. Apparently, they produced a favourable report because the American government paid Ginter for his venture into Alaska. Ginter admired the agents' professionalism.

Someone once asked Ben Ginter why he had chosen Prince George for his base of operation, and he answered because it is located in the centre of the province. He hinted, as far as Ben was capable of "hinting" anything, that he had been certain from the first day he arrived in 1949 that the town had a great future and that he was going to play a large role in that future. Ginter was not boasting. He became an ambassador for Prince George and "put it on the map" as he liked to say.

Former Lands, Forest and Water Resources Minister and Fort George MLA Ray Williston said Ginter's choice of Prince George was not altogether altruistic and when Ginter first came to the Interior city, he had no intentions of staying to make the city the headquarters of his operations. It was just another stop of a basically itinerant contractor who would go where the jobs were. It just so happened that Prince George became an important place in the development of the province's North. Ginter had the right instinct to put down roots.

"Ginter was never accepted in the Vancouver Club circle, where the movers and shakers of British Columbia ruled. To them Ginter was an uneducated bumpkin, and Ginter was aware of the feeling. In Vancouver he was a small fish in a large pond," Williston said, "Ginter chose Prince George because he could be a big fish in a much smaller pond, which suited Ginter just fine."

Ben hits the news. This collage of various newspaper articles is only a small sampling of the headlines that followed him throughout his career.

Not all of his work for the reputation of the city was positive, and many residents felt embarrassed by Ginter's actions which more often than not resulted in glaring headlines in the provincial press. It hurt Ginter that people in Prince George did not take to him. He had spread the name of the city throughout Canada, always stating that he came from Prince George and what a good place that city was. He had built a showplace home on the city's outskirts and assured everyone he was proud to be from the Central Interior's major city. Some people were not sure that Ginter's promotion of Prince George was an altogether good thing, as Ben Ginter had become famous, or infamous as some preferred, not only in British Columbia but throughout Canada and even internationally. His name most often was linked with law suits and court actions. Ginter would sue an opponent or competitors at the drop of a hat if he felt he had been slighted or unfairly taken advantage of. Ben was also known to quarrel publicly with governments and big labour. All in all, his was a reputation many people in Prince George felt uneasy about when it was linked to that of their city.

Ginter's personality would brook no opposition. He would set a target for himself and go after it. Opponents would be brow-beaten or taken to court. Not many could stand up to Ginter's forceful ways. He became dedicated to the principles that all opposition, whether by governments, unions or competitors was bad, and that entrepreneurs like him should be allowed to write their own rules. There was one exception from that dedication, however. Government was not bad as long as it furthered his own interests. In other words, over the years Ginter had become extremely reactionary in his views.

It was rumoured in the early 1970s that he had become a member of the right-wing Republican Party of Canada, but Ginter always denied this. He did take a stab at politics in British Columbia in 1972. The president of the Liberal Party of B.C., Mel Couvelier, approached Ginter to run for the leadership of the party. Two others were in the race: Member of Parliament David Anderson and Surrey Mayor William Vander Zalm. Couvelier later switched from the Liberal party to the Socreds and became finance minister in the cabinet of another former Liberal, the same Bill Vander Zalm, who became premier of British Columbia in 1986. Anderson won after Ginter withdrew because of lack of support. Ginter's assessment of his two opponents was that

Anderson was a seasoned politician and rather "crafty." He described Vander Zalm as a man without depths, a "very shallow person."

Ginter's only other attempt to enter public life happened when he ran for a seat on Prince George city council. He ended up sixth in a field of six candidates. This attempt to enter local politics was less an effort to help run the city than to test his local popularity once again.

His perceived preference of the Socreds was finally shattered by these events. People had always believed Ginter was a Socred. They were wrong. He saw the Bennett government and Highways Minister Gaglardi as nothing more than a springboard for his ambitions and a way to make money. He was rather detached from the party line and the philosophy of Social Credit. When he was no longer regarded as the golden-haired road builder, he blamed the party and the individual Socreds for his misfortune; and his friendship with Gaglardi soured when major construction projects were hard to find. The boom had slowed down although roads were still being built. Ginter was one of the first to feel this slowdown. Socred supporters no longer liked his ambivalence.

7

GINTER WAS LOOKING FOR NEW FIELDS to conquer. He needed a new challenge. Ginter was a great initiator but always lost interest once he achieved his goal. It was the chase that interested him rather than the catch.

The world's need for pulp products had grown enormously, and British Columbia was building pulp mills everywhere, including three in Prince George. Ginter was no longer content to just clear sites for new mills. He wanted to be part of the industry. He startled the industry and the public when he offered $12 million for a timber licence to harvest trees in the Peace River Basin. The original bidder, Cattermole Timber Limited of Vancouver, had offered the government the upset price of $340,000 for the same timber. Ginter's bid hit the industry like a bombshell. Cries of "piracy" and "chicanery" were heard.

Cattermole had not expected any opposition when it bid the upset price for the 18,800 square mile area in the Finlay Forest Reserve. Ginter made the huge bid to assure himself a lasting timber supply for the pulp mill he planned to build. He said he wanted to construct a three-hundred-ton-a-day mill and submitted a personal cheque in the amount of the upset price. This price was the estimated value of the timber for harvest. Ginter's offer included the upset price, but topped the Cattermole bid by offering the government another $12.6 million over a period of twenty-one years for the timber rights.

"This is absolutely ridiculous," cried Richard Cattermole, president of the low bidding company. An agreement had been reached earlier between the provincial government and Cattermole, which recognized the company as the applicant for the rights. Forest Minister Ray Williston hurriedly agreed to give Cattermole an extra ten days to match Ginter's bid. Ginter protested at once, but Williston stuck to his agreement. Ginter had long had his eyes on that timber. He believed a pulp mill would be a good venture to replace his sagging highways construction business. When Williston set up the Crown timber areas in the summer of 1964 to give Cattermole and Alexandra Forest Industries Ltd. first chance at the rights, Ginter kept quiet but followed developments closely.

Cattermole and Alexandra had been competing for the same harvesting region until Williston made it possible for both to proceed with pulp mills. Alexandra had specified a special area in which it was seeking harvesting rights. When bids were opened in Victoria, Alexandra was the sole bidder, offering $460,000 for a twenty-one year licence. Williston accepted the offer.

Cattermole had sought the rights for an area next to Alexandra's, but was blown out of the water by Ginter's surprise bid. At first Cattermole was unsure whether to match the rival bid. Ginter said his offer of extras to the government was not out of line. He insisted Cattermole should not be given extra time to regroup and match his bid.

Williston was in a quandary. He could not ignore Ginter's bid, but he had to adhere to the agreements reached earlier in the year with Cattermole, a company which had one advantage: it was an established firm. Ginter said he would incorporate a new company before December 31, 1964, the government's deadline. "We could clear a site about one hundred miles north of Prince George within one year," Ginter said. He was confident he would be able to produce three hundred tons of pulp daily by December 31, 1970, the deadline the government imposed.

"I am not concerned about all that," he told the press. One of his companies, Grace Finance, had already conducted a preliminary survey, and his backing would come from Canadian and American sources, Ginter stated, but he did not identify his backers. Just before Cattermole's extra ten days of grace expired, his company matched Ginter's bid. It included several reservations which Williston said he had to study before accepting. A few days later the minister said his legal advice was that Cattermole had met "without equivocation the rival bid, but I am seeking assurance Cattermole understood all stipulations of a new agreement."

When Cattermole asked for another extension to study all legal aspects, Ginter protested again. Williston ignored the protests. He agreed, however, to keep Ginter's cheque until the situation was clarified. This left Ben with at least some hope for eventual success. When the agreement was finally signed, the government returned Ginter's check. He had lost the bid. But at that time Ginter was no longer interested, anyway. In 1965 he had found a way to get his own pulp mill at Kitimat.

He had been informed that a consortium of Finnish companies

had shown interest in investing in Canada's pulp industry. Ginter at once went to Finland and came back a winner. The Finns formed a consortium consisting of Enso-Gutzeit Osakeythio, a company largely owned by the Finnish government; Kymin Osakeythio-Kynmene Aktiebolag; Myllykosken Paperitehas Oy, and Oy Tampella AB to set up Eurocan Pulp and Paper Company Limited. Ginter and ten Terrace area sawmill owners also became partners. While finances had all been set, the granting of the licence for timber harvesting and a tree farm was hotly contested by Crown Zellerbach and MacMillan Bloedel, the province's forest industry giants. Eurocan won at a hearing in Kitimat, and Ginter was chosen as president of the new firm. It was a personal triumph for him when Lands, Forest and Water Resources Minister Ray Williston turned a bucket of earth, signalling the start of constructing the hundred-million-dollar mill. Skeptics maintained there was not enough timber in the area to sustain a mill. In his usual direct way, Ginter replied to his critics, "There's no reason to believe there isn't any timber, because there is." He stayed on as president until 1969. In 1970 he sold his fifteen per cent in the company to the original Finnish investors "for a tidy profit." That was all he would ever say publicly about the sale of his shares.

In the beginning, Ginter's construction company was hired to to clear the site for the mill, but this project was troubled from the start. Machine operators complained Ginter had sent inferior equipment to the sites, and considerable time was wasted repairing machinery instead of having it work. Again, Ginter had union problems. The men involved in this $100 million project were members of the International Brotherhood of Teamsters, the International Union of

Operating Engineers Local 115, and the Labourers Union. They lived in a construction camp near the mill site.

The standard contract between Ben Ginter Construction Company Limited and the unions on the job called for Ginter to provide a bus service from the camp to the work site if the distance exceeded three miles. For shorter distances, the men had to find their own way to work. Ginter stuck to the letter of the contract when the Kitimat workers demanded a shuttle service, as the Riverview Camp was two-tenths of a mile short of the required three-mile distance. Given the rainy weather on the coast and the muddy road leading to the work site, the men expected Ginter would prove to be understanding and provide a bus. No way, Ginter said, read the contract. He did not even want to talk to the shop stewards or other union representatives about the problem. As far as he was concerned, there was no problem. Unrest and discontent spread among the workers and rumours of possible work stoppages circulated. Ginter countered by delivering a pre-emptive blow. He fired all teamsters and had their draglines moved off the job.

"We did not really know what was happening," a union official recalled.

The men got together and decided to withhold their services, another name for an illegal strike. Ginter immediately took action. He condemned the workers' action as an illegal walkout and said the sixty-seven men had been working on the site for two months before the dispute arose. Why were they suddenly complaining about the lack of transportation? Union officials countered that the men's grievances were an accumulation of problems over those two months. Ginter announced he was going to hire non-union workers, and anyone who wanted to work could have a job. Less than ten men answered his call. Ginter cut back to one shift. Cutting out the second shift would not delay the project, Ginter said, adding "all we are concerned with is the work on the building site so we can start driving piles."

Union officials reluctantly admit today that Ginter had the law on his side. They still cannot understand why he was so bull-headed over the lacking two-tenths of a mile needed for bus service. The only explanation seems to be that Ginter located the camp deliberately short of the distance required by the contract because he knew he could not handle the site-clearing project, but was too proud to back out. Therefore, he deliberately provoked a fight with the unions so that he could claim they lost him the work. Ginter, although he was a shareholder in the mill, would not budge. The workers would not lessen their demands either, and as a result the men walked off the job.

Ginter threatened law suits and applied for court injunctions, but he could not get anyone to return to work. When Eurocan officials became worried about meeting construction deadlines and asked Ginter to solve the problem or withdraw from the project, Ginter capitulated and withdrew his construction firm as the site preparation contractor. He turned over the job to Marwell Construction of Vancouver.

In retrospect the Kitimat bus incident may not have evolved into a major event, if Ginter were not involved. Organized labour hated his guts. It did not matter which union was involved, as Ginter liked to fight them all. It was not the only time Ginter would be asked asked to leave a major job. Later, in 1973, the International Union of Operating Engineers was on strike against

Kelfor's Houston Mining Limited project where Ginter was the major contractor. Attempts to settle were made by face-to-face negotiations. The meetings failed to get the workers back to their jobs. The union, seeing Ginter would not budge, declared it would picket every job of Ben Ginter Construction Company Limited. When the Houston strike started in November, the workers had been without a collective agreement since August. They wanted retroactive pay.

Ginter personally conducted part of the negotiations. He agreed to keep negotiating until a settlement was reached because two days earlier Northwood Pulp and Timber Limited had asked him to vacate a job at their Prince George site. Ginter's company had been building new effluent lagoons at the mill's site. Northwood was concerned that anti-Ginter picket lines could shut down the pulp mill. Northwood could not afford a shutdown and asked Ginter to leave the project.

His dislike of unions stemmed from his disgust with what he saw as weakness. He believed sincerely that anyone could make his own way in the world without having to join a group and let someone else speak for him. He considered those who banded together as weak. Ginter, who professed not to be anti-union, nevertheless felt that big unions were as bad for freewheelers like him as were big government. He despised union organizers who, he said, were better working with their mouths than with their tools. He thought of them as "red" agitators, although he did not mind some of them personally. Ginter, in turn, was viewed by labour as a man who would do his utmost to keep the working-man in his place in a sort of patriarchal relationship of "you just do what I tell you and I'll look after you."

Moving the earth. Ginter's machinery clears a site for pulp mill construction.

Such an attitude was no longer good enough for workers in British Columbia with its boom-time developments. Not only did the workers want their share of prosperity through good wages, but also they wanted to do a job in greater comfort with less effort. And why not, the unions argued, everyone was trying to make as good a living as possible. It was a totally alien attitude to Ginter. Whenever he saw something that did not comply with

GINTER

his work ethic, he tried to stop it by any means. That often meant taking the perceived offenders to court. He launched million-dollar law suits against some unions and against some individual union officials. Recalling that he once had been sued for a half-million dollars because Ginter believed he had incited workers to walk off their jobs, Howard German, a building trades unions official, said, "Ginter was the best trainer for union business agents. If they could survive a bargaining session with Ginter, they could survive bargaining with anyone."

Suing a union was no idle sport for Ginter. He knew it would cost him money. He also knew that the unions would incur heavy expenses when he dragged them into court. Ginter often played for time in his dealings with unions and filing legal action sometimes bought him this time. This did not only apply to his dealings with organized labour; his reliance on the courts was evident in many of his other dealings.

Ben Ginter had a great turnover of legal representatives. If a lawyer was unable to win for Ginter, the lawyer was liable to be fired on the spot. On the other hand, Ginter did not seem to have much respect for the courts and their rulings. One time he had been sued for failing to pay a major bill and was hauled before the judge. After hearing the case, the court found Ginter guilty and ordered him to pay his bill. When the court recessed the plaintiff walked over to Ginter and asked when he could expect to receive a cheque. "What cheque?" Ginter asked.

"The one for the amount we just won in this courtroom," the other man said. Ginter looked him straight into the eyes.

Without showing any emotion he simply said, "Sue me," and walked out.

Most of his legal battles resulted in monetary losses. Ginter did not seem to mind. If he believed he was right, he would fight to the end regardless of costs. Ben believed his moral convictions were worth the losses. Not that he set out to lose when he initiated legal action: he was certain that logic and clear thinking — as he saw it — would prevail on his side. The reasons for his losses could be found in government and legal bureaucracy, Ginter said. He detested both. Ginter's legal actions were by no means necessarily small or frivolous. He sued Canadian National Railways for so much money that the House of Parliament set up an inquiry, and Ginter managed to speak personally with the Speaker in chambers in Ottawa. The eventual hearings took place in Winnipeg and lasted for more than four weeks.

While Ginter viewed lawyers as parasites, he was unable to get along without them. He saw them as people making money from the misery of others however contributing nothing or very little to the welfare of mankind. Any lawyer who would not act exactly as Ginter had instructed would find himself looking for other clients. On occasion Ginter went as far as dismissing lawyers right in the courtroom before the judge retired from the courtroom.

In one incident, an examination for discovery, Ginter took over questioning of a witness when he felt his lawyer was not asking the right questions. It was highly embarrassing for this respected member of the legal profession but there was nothing he could do. He resigned as Ginter's lawyer soon after, needless to say. The resignation did not matter to Ginter; he hired new legal representation. To him, lawyers were plentiful, and many were eager to be hired in spite of his reputation. His battle with the lawyers had its lighter side. The students at the University of British Columbia law school felt it was time Ginter should be recognized for his 'contributions' to lawyers and they made him an 'honorary lawyer.' This caused much dismay and consternation among the university's law faculty and the provincial bar association. While those two august bodies took the matter seriously, Ginter took it in stride and with good humour, knowing it was a hoax. Playing along with the students gave him the last laugh.

8

Ben Ginter could not understand why he was disliked in Prince George. Had he not re-opened the brewery? Had he not rescued the annual fall fair from certain death? Had he not built a house of a kind never before seen in the North? Had he not won honours with his prize Arabian horses? Had he not always mentioned he came from Prince George, wherever he was? And most of all, had he not provided employment for a large number of local residents? Did he not, at Christmas time, contribute to the Christmas spirit by hitching a horse to a red sled and have it driven around town to deliver Santa Claus to special Christmas functions?

Of course, he also used the sled to take a few cases of beer to friends during that time. Each year his beer boxes displayed a holiday motif and the sled's appearance was popular. He knew people were envious of his achievements and it made him bitter. He compared his treatment by Prince George with that he received in Red Deer, Alberta. He said that his Fuddle Duck wine in Alberta outsold his combined wine sales in British Columbia. He felt his mentioning of Prince George wherever he appeared was of great value for the town.

"Whenever I ask what people know about Prince George, they say pulp mills and Ben Ginter," he once said. He found the newcomers to Prince George quite friendly but could not understand the attitude of old-time residents. He said he tried to do his bit by bringing industry to Prince George and that his construction company was the largest in the province with a payroll unmatched by any other company in the city. He wondered if he would not have been better off being an ordinary Cat operator. This, he said, would have given him more time to spend with his family and friends. It was not that he really needed the support of the people of Prince George, but it hurt him that a town like Red Deer, where he had done nothing but constructed a brewery, would treat him so well, while Prince George, where he had done so much, gave him the cold shoulder.

"In Red Deer they have not forgotten what I was trying to do," he said. They also remembered that he was bringing in Canadian industry with Canadian dollars which resulted in high employment for the people and increased revenue to the city. He was recognized for this, he said. But in Prince George and in Kitimat, he could not find that kind of recognition. He was furious with Kitimat because he had brought the Eurocan pulp mill to that coastal city and was still waiting for any kind of recognition from the city fathers and the people of Kitimat. It never occurred to Ginter that he may have been partially at fault. He blamed envy or jealousy for the lack of gratitude. In Ben's mind, there wasn't a club, an organization or a church he had not contributed to. His lack of recognition was galling.

What really upset Ginter was the Prince George Chamber of Commerce had been asked to submit a brief to an inquiry by a

Royal Commission into the liquor industry, but Mayor Harold Moffat refused to support this submission that backed up several of Ginter's suggestions for changes in this industry. The commission had been set up by the provincial government because of increasing complaints from the public, retail outlets, and even manufacturers about the way liquor was sold and promoted in the province.

The mayor had his own ideas about liquor, and he was not about to become a party to things he did not believe in by supporting the chamber's brief, thereby supporting Ben. Ginter always said he would have liked to have known why the locals did not support him. He said he must have done something but could not figure out what it was he had done. Everywhere else, Ginter said, he was recognized. He was invited to ride in the Calgary Stampede parade, the Red Deer parade, as well as take part in the Klondike Days in Edmonton. Invitations to civic festivals in Winnipeg and Swan River also flowed in. He was awarded a trophy in the Pacific National Exhibition parade as the best single rider. He received national coverage on radio and television. Each time he mentioned Prince George. It made not a difference to Prince George residents.

When Ginter became involved, the Prince George Exhibition/Fall Fair was not doing well financially. Attendance was down and money was short. Ginter raised beautiful Hereford cattle and Arabian horses on his ranch, winning prizes all over western Canada and the northwestern United States. Ginter liked to show off his prize possessions and many people enjoyed seeing his outstanding livestock. He had found an ideal spot to exhibit his animals. Fair officials were glad to have Ben Ginter on board

General George R. Pearkes, VC, B.C. Lieutenant Governor, and Ben Ginter swap stories at the Prince George Exhibition in 1962.

and usually — but not always — he had his special stalls at the the fair in Prince George. Each year he brought his livestock down from the ranch.

Grace Ginter was closely involved in this part of her husband's life, for it was she who was responsible for getting the animals ready for show. Ginter had hired some people from northern Europe to be in charge of his livestock, but Grace liked working with animals. Come fair time, the stock securely down at the site, Ginter would don his big cowboy hat and put on his shiny cowboy boots. Then he would go out into the grounds and hold court. He would push his hat back, put one arm over the top rail, sling his foot on the lowest rung and talk to people. He really enjoyed the attention and talking.

Meanwhile, back at the barn, his wife and hired hands would be getting the animals ready for the show. They often won blue ribbons because they did have first class stock. Ginter did not like it when he did not win or when he was not assigned the stalls he wanted. One year he got so angry he withdrew from the fair before anyone had a chance to talk to him. Shortly thereafter he called city hall and offered to buy the fair grounds. He was willing to pay any reasonable price for it. Asked what he was going to do with it, Ginter angrily informed civic authorities he was going to turn the grounds into a cow pasture. The city did not sell him the land, and Ginter's association with the fall fair ended.

Ben Ginter was one of the first people who kept Arabian horses, but the first horses of this breed were brought to Prince George by Stan Carling, provincial government agent, and John Coates, a local lawyer. As government agent, Carling often dealt with Ginter officially. Any town over five thousand had a govern-

Ben proudly displays Bini Binis, a full-blooded Arabian stallion, a 1965 Grand Champion.

ment agent who was the senior civil servant for that town and its surrounding area. It was a powerful position. The agent distributed cheques for work done on government contracts. He usually fulfilled the offices of justice of the peace as well as of coroner, collector of property taxes, gold commissioner, marriage commissioner, head of the local assessment authority, citizenship judge, and manager of the motor vehicle branch. Ginter's companies had numerous vehicles, and Ben often went to the government to get licences issued by the motor vehicle branch.

He often talked with Carling and they found a mutual interest in horses. As they got to know each other better, they socialized and talked Arabians. Soon they exhibited their horses together at various shows. Carling's first experience with Ginter's egotism occurred when they had taken their horses to Salem, Oregon for a show. Ginter had his stallion and Carling had a mare in the events. The mare was slightly injured in the ring, and Carling withdrew her from further showings. Ginter expressed his concern about the animal and repeated it often over the next four days. "That poor horse, you have to have it looked after."

"That poor horse, you should leave it here because you can't transport an injured animal that far."

"What are you going to do with this poor horse?"

Carling found it quite disconcerting and finally asked Ginter why he was so concerned, as the injury was not that serious. Ginter made a few evasions before Carling discovered that Ben had bought another horse in Salem, and he wanted to take it to Prince George. Since they had travelled to the show in a two-horse trailer, Ginter no longer wanted to take Carling's horse back. Carling had to return with Ginter to British Columbia leaving the mare behind, then take his own trailer and return to Oregon to pick up his mare and drive it back to Prince George.

"Ben did not give a damn about me or my horse; he did not bother to tell me about buying another horse, but made it look as if I was not treating my mare properly by wanting to take it home the way we came," Carling said. "It was an act of pure selfishness." Relations between the two men cooled off considerably after that, but they kept in touch until Ginter's death.

"Looking back," said Carling, now retired, "Ginter was the most self-centred person I had ever known, and the only reason

Ginter seemed to have sought my company was that I presented a challenge; he could not control me. Ben needed to control people and he needed to be the first and best in everything."

Carling described a tour to Alberta when a number of people went with Ginter on a duck hunt. Sitting in the cabins after dark, the men played a few hands of poker, with Ginter always the winner. Carling did not believe Ginter was such a great poker player but said Ben would buy the pots. "He could outbid all the others because he carried way more cash with him. How could you do this to your friends?"

But Carling admired Ginter for his astuteness in business. "No one, not even the greatest expert in his own field, could pull the wool over Ben's eyes. Ben had a brain like a computer and could pick up details and facts in the matter of minutes. In this, he was one of the smartest men I have ever known," Carling said.

It was Ginter's lack of concern for others that bothered Carling. "He hired me one day to take a horse to a show in Vancouver. I asked only that he pay my expenses and he agreed. When the day came on which I was to pick up the horse, Ginter did not phone. I finally called him and asked what was going on. Ben told me he had made other arrangements. It did not matter to him that I had cancelled everything else and was waiting for his call."

An incident related by a Prince George businessman shows Ginter's lack of a sense of humour when the prank was played on him. Ginter and three hunters set out one morning to shoot a few ducks. Ginter sported a brand new ten-gallon hat much to the amusement of his fellow hunters. It appeared the ducks did not want to become targets that morning and the hunters grew rather bored. One grabbed Ginter's hat and flung it into the air. Another drew a bead on it and pulled the trigger. The beautiful Stetson disintegrated. Ginter was not amused and immediately left the blind the men were hiding in. He got into his vehicle, the only one the men brought along and took off without speaking a word to his friends. They were forced to walk back to civilization, a long walk. They never went hunting with Ginter again.

Ginter wrote the following open letter to the citizens of Prince George in 1972:

"I am just going to tell you in the place when I bid and was successful bidder on the brewery, I did not buy it to reactivate it as a brewery, but the citizens of Prince George came to me — the mayor and others — asking me to reactivate this brewery. They said 'We will support you, we will buy your beer — this is the only secondary industry in Prince George and you have enough money to be able to reactivate it, and money isn't everything, you are a Prince George citizen and how about keeping this secondary industry going and keeping some employment in the area — they are good people that worked down there and you won't regret it.

I want to explain to you . . . I am not interested in the glory or the satisfaction of saying that I own a brewery in Prince George or own a house I may be proud of and anyone who is successful has to be proud with the people he lives with and gives work to and that brewery, to me, belongs to Prince George and not to me or anyone else. That is the reason I am going public now that the Social Credit government is out and now I have permission to go public at the fastest possible speed.

I detest and hate people who are selfish and make hogs of themselves and don't share with others.

I don't think anyone, as far as I am concerned, can accuse me of this because I take little out of life when it comes to the way I live. I am not a big spender, or one of the last big spenders. It happens to the contrary. I look after myself not nearly enough according to my doctor and according to the people who work around me.

They can't understand this type of endurance, how I work the hours I do with no proper vacations and don't take time for my family and recreation. Now, the old saying is still there, in the end I realize and appreciate being told that 'I can't take it with me.' I have often remarked 'then I am not going.' But, people nearly every day ask me, 'What are you working for — you have everything you want. Why shorten your life because people are not going to give you credit for it or could care less if you do or if you don't.'

People suggest that I have all kinds of money. These are only really monetary things and I cannot eat money, cannot sleep it or enjoy it when I am working. Money is the necessary evil that gives me the tools to be able to do the things which I am trying to do for people that I feel deserve to have the best when it comes to things in life.

In the North, more things could be accomplished if they did not think so much of their own self and a little bit more than they are doing for their fellow man, whether he is a janitor, a ditch digger, hippy, or whatever he is. He is a human being and don't always worry about that guy who is not doing anything, or who is becoming rich, as they call it, because you are able to enjoy this richness.

If some of us are more capable or more gifted or are more prepared or have more self-discipline — you have to have self-discipline yourself to continue to keep anything in spite of what anyone might say. Look at the people who run public life — how much thanks do they get whether they become premier or prime minister, alderman, or mayor. The only thing I wish they would remember when they reach their goal is that they would not forget the people that put them there as from what I have seen there's always a 'before and after.'

Before becoming prime minister, for example, they are common people who will speak to the common people and after they are out of office they again become common people who will speak to the common people of every walk of life. As for me leaving Prince George and as for me building a brewery in Vancouver, this may have eventually happened, anyway.

But I must say that this is the attitude of a lot of people here in Prince George that has advanced my project in Richmond sooner and I hope that when the project is finished that I still have enough market in the north not to have to close the brewery in Prince George.

I can assure you that I cannot any longer subsidize or carry a payroll in the north country as during our last negotiations we could have come to no agreement but a complete shut-down of the brewery at that time or parity with the coast as these were the demands by the men of the union. I had to meet these demands — subsidize a subsidy.

I do admit everyone can only ask so much and that once in a while you like to have a pat on the back rather than a kick in the pants for what you are trying to do.

Who benefits most from this . . . myself, my family, my relations or the people? Our market after all is in Vancouver from the economic point of view.

It is not possible for me to continue to produce a product here where I have to bring the raw material in and take them back to the coast for marketing. This is only common sense.

While I am marketing at the coast the big breweries and monopolies are cross-hauling and bringing in their product down here and, if anything, I feel our product, especially the water is superior to any product on the market. This is what we are told by the top laboratory in North America who tests everybody's brew. We even had these compliments all the way from Europe and, after all, the Europeans are the oldest in the brewing industry.

I feel our brew-master, deceased, and his brother who is presently our production manager and brew-master, are the finest and the best the world has ever brought to this industry and no brewery in North America will argue this point. If anybody thinks they are feathering my nest by buying my product, well, they better think again whether they are feathering my nest or their own.

As far as the construction work is concerned, I have no immediate plan of moving the construction company out of Prince George. We have as many contracts as anyone now, but as you know Bennett (Premier w.a.c.) either kept the money in the pot or else started building two railways parallelling one another into 'no man's land' when it difficult to get people to work in Prince George. How are we supposed to subsidize that type of project?

Sure, I appreciate we got some work from the building of that railway but that does not alter my feelings from an economic point of view of building that railway which is running all the way to Cassiar. Maintenance alone is going to be millions and millions every year and it is the taxpayers' money that is going to pay for it.

People should concern themselves about better roads and better recreational facilities and things of this nature in order to encourage more technical and skilled people to move to the Prince George area or the northern part of British Columbia which is already opened up, but not nearly fully enough developed or hardly touched. This floundering all over the country building trails and roads in the bush is not going to get us anywhere.

I am positive that this new government is going to take a serious look at the present situation to see whether the tax dollars are squandered and spent with no return for this generation, at least.

I think I have done much in helping Prince George recreational facilities through donations and investment as any other industry in Prince George . . . also the churches, clubs, and various sports. The people seem to have a very short memory when it comes to these things. Give them a few thousand dollars today and tomorrow they have forgotten that they even heard about you.

But I am not begging for a living and not begging the

people to support me — only bringing this to your attention now that the issue has been raised why I should be leaving Prince George.

You will admit everybody has feelings and I have feelings, too and they run deep, even if many people may not agree.

As far as the citizens of the Prince George area are concerned, I think I am one of the biggest taxpayers, but I get no work from the City of Prince George and what I get would not pay my light or water bill — let alone the sewers.

I asked the people of Prince George when they have seen us getting any city work around here except on a couple of occasions which is a drop in the bucket. Sometimes when they cannot rent equipment anywhere else they will rent the odd grader from us to do some snow-plowing but the hotel and banks who cash our pay-cheques will have to agree that there is a lot of payroll brought into Prince George by our companies.

In spite of this I still think there is a lot of nice people in Prince George and I am not suggesting that everybody has the same feelings toward me. I came here in 1949 and watched this city grow from a bud to the blossom it is today.

I am very proud of Prince George and have never hesitated wherever I travelled across the world to say I came from Prince George, even if most people say 'where is that — is that way up north?' Well, I am proud to be from way up north and proud of the people that developed and helped it grow to what it is today.

I may have fired many people in my lifetime, but still those same people that I fired, I understand them and care as much for them as I do for the next guy, but I usually try to make everybody pull their own weight and whenever I found anyone that wasn't, I had not time for them.

Maybe, I often got them at the wrong time as they said to me on one of the contracts 'We don't know, yesterday everything was running smoothly and today everything is going wrong.' But looking at the figures I think they were stretching it a bit.

I feel that no one can understand the workingman better than me because I came from the bottom and as far as I am concerned, I do not hesitate, at any time, to go back to the bottom to speak to the people who are working.

Not everybody can be a millionaire and I repeat, that regardless of what you do, as long as you do something and do it well so you can be proud of what you do, you are doing as much or maybe more.

I wish we all could be millionaires, but I don't think that would be practical, feasible, or possible."

Ginter wrote this letter in 1972 but no one knows what he was going to do with it. Parts of the letter have been quoted in various articles before, but his statements give a good insight into the man; he was human after all.

This letter was Ben's state-of-the-union letter. It sums up Ben quite well. He uses the carrot and the stick; he appeals and threatens. He wants to show he can be understanding but, at the same time, he sets himself apart by referring to his wealth. He wants a pat on the back because he feels he deserves it. He refers to his humble beginning only to point out his considerable achievements that set him apart from others. The use of the plural "us" in referring to himself is telling.

He says he is not really interested in money, then negates this statement by threatening to pull out of Prince George if he is unable to make more money. Aside from the threats and appeals, Ginter is crying for acceptance in the letter. He wants to be loved, or if not loved, at least not be hated or jealously envied. Citing the benefit his brewery and house brought to the city, he then complains he cannot get city work. He accuses the union local of not supporting him and uses this as an excuse to speed up his withdrawal from the city to the Lower Mainland. He was not to blame for the move; lack of local support forced him, Ginter says in this letter. He was right, of course, that his main market was in the Vancouver area because that's the main population centre of the province.

In this letter, Ginter portrays himself as one who endures much but complains, at the same time, that he does not take vacations, but he vows to continue his way of life. He scoffs at his own wealth and says it is only a tool to help others, the very same others he admits having fired because they did not measure up to his standards. Ginter points to what he contributes to charity but says he is not begging. However, that is exactly what he is doing.

9

ALTHOUGH HE ADMITS THAT HIS FEELINGS were hurt in Prince George, it does not occur to him that maybe some of the reasons he found his feeling hurt were his attitude and the cavalier way he paid his bills. He blames others because he cannot see himself as having done anything wrong; it would have never entered his mind. Ginter's entreaties would have evoked only yawns even if the majority of Prince George residents had learned about the letter, not that they did. Ginter had threatened too often to pull out and move to the coast. It held no threat to Prince George because everyone knew Ginter was already living in the Lower Mainland most of the time.

Ginter had some other definite ideas about life and he was outspoken about them: "Man always works best under pressure," he said, "Look back at your history. As far back as you can see, it seems wars have always brought out the best in us. Now we are getting fat and lazy and nobody is cultivated or trained or schooled enough — the politicians especially — to know how to survive in peacetime. Here you have politicians, people who could not make a go of it running a private business, and here you have

Ginter with Robert Stanfield in Winnipeg during the 1968 federal election. Ginter loaned his plane to Stanfield to fly around Canada during the campaign.

them running the biggest business in the country, the government. It doesn't make any sense.

"If I," Ben Ginter said, "could make one contribution in this life, I would like to fight for the youth of today and of tomorrow. They are subjected to things that don't make any sense. The things we are doing are so backward. We are allowing kids to quit school at fifteen, uneducated and untrained. A kid like that is not mature enough to handle life. The unions give him big money and he gets the idea that, because of union security, he can't be fired. He's ruined. If government and business had any real feeling for kids today, they'd make it compulsory that, if a kid quits school at fifteen or so, he would have to take another two years of some kind of training. Give them some choice but have the decision on training made by some panel and based on aptitude. Then you wouldn't have so many young people go off on the wrong foot."

As for himself, Ginter said, he made his way without pandering to politicians. "I made my pile without chucking dough into the Social Credit slush fund," he said. This did not mean he would not curry political favours such as letting Robert Stanfield, the leader of the Progressive Conservative Party of Canada, use his aircraft in western Canada when Stanfield ran for prime minister in 1968.

Ginter explained he did not belong to clubs because he did not have the time, and he was not inclined toward that type of recreation. He had let his membership in several Prince George service clubs lapse for that reason.

"I am addicted to work in the same way some other people are addicted to alcohol," he said.

Ben Ginter did have his reflective moments and sometimes he was prophetic. In 1971, a time when nobody thought or cared much about the environment, Ginter called for a tax on pollution. He suggested the federal government set up a sliding tax on industries who create the greatest pollution problems. The way he saw it, the money collected from the tax could be used finance a nation-wide waste management program.

"This tax would be assessed and collected at the federal level from manufacturers and distributed to provincial authorities who

Grace Ginter and her sons
Shane, centre, and James,
left, on a stroll in Vancouver
after they left Prince George.

qualify by reason of their co-operation in accepting the program,"
he suggested. He proposed a recycling system especially for
bottles, cans and paper cartons which would require a central
body of highly qualified specialists in waste management. This
central agency would be active in all municipalities and would
collect all kinds of litter for recycling. This law, he said, should not
be directed toward the individual litterbug, but at the wholesale
producers of waste. At another time Ginter addressed a professional women's club and warned that in the not-so-distant future,
a double income family would be the norm rather than the
exception. This was in the late 1960s when most women were
looking after home and family, but Ginter said increasing cost of
all necessities would force many more women into the labour
force.

A rare shot of Ben and son Shane at the beach in Mexico.

At the time his self-serving letter was written, Ben Ginter was a lonely man. His wife Grace and his two sons, James and Shane, were no longer living with him. He was living in a hotel suite in Vancouver and did not exactly look after himself. His once trim body had turned to flab and was dominated by a huge belly. Grace Ginter and her sons had left Prince George in 1968. To her, there was no use in living with Ben any longer, since he hardly spent any time at all with his family and did not talk to them when he was home.

Ginter had never been much of a family man. He did not spend much time with his sons when they grew older, although when they were younger, the family went on flying fishing trips in one of Ginter's aircraft. Ginter demanded much of those around him, and his sons were no exception when he was home. He sometimes teased the boys so unmercifully that some friends said this teasing was close to physical abuse. One time he threw his youngest son, a good swimmer, into the pool at his house, but was forced to dive in fully clothed to pull him out. The boy was in shock, as he had not expected this treatment.

After spending the first school years at a Prince George elementary school, James Ginter was enrolled in a private school in Vancouver. Ben insisted Shane also go to a private school after his mother had moved from Prince George.

Ginter also liked to go hunting and fishing, but mostly was too busy to indulge in the few hobbies he had. There was a darker side to Ben Ginter that was apparent to some of the people who were close to the family who would never talk about it. Grace Ginter sometimes had a black eye which she hid behind sunglasses, never revealing what happened to her. Ben Ginter had also become a womanizer. It was common knowledge in Prince George, and possibly elsewhere, that he had a roving eye. Some people who attended parties at his house on Cranbrook Hill report they were shocked to hear Ginter say to any woman who caught his fancy that she had never been bedded until she had been bedded by him. Those who overheard Ben saying something like that always hoped his wife would not be aware of it. If she was, Grace Ginter never let on.

It was no secret that when he discovered one of his employees had an attractive wife, he would invite the couple to fly to Reno or Las Vegas with him in the company aircraft. If they agreed, Ginter would suddenly find that the husband was absolutely needed on some job-site to solve a problem. When asked about the trip, Ginter would shrug his shoulders and say it could not be avoided, the man would have to do some troubleshooting for him. However, since he was going, he might as well take the wife along, since she was all prepared to go. Sometimes this ploy worked to the regret of the husband involved.

Ginter's notoriety was such that some people disliked him without really knowing why. His reputation predisposed people, even in innocence, to dislike him. A prominent Prince George woman, born in Germany, disliked him because her husband had told her Ginter was a "cat-skinner." This woman had problems with the English language and still thought in German. When she was informed about what Ginter did, she took it literally. Here was a man who skinned cats for a living. When her husband told her about Ginter's occupation, she asked a few questions such as where did he work, who hired him and what sort of tools he was using.

The husband, not thinking about his wife's limited knowledge of English, patiently explained in rather vague terms, which did not help her to get a clear picture. Knowing his reputation, she decided right then that she would never talk to Ginter. After being invited to one of the parties at the Ginter house, she went but made good on her resolve. She ignored him and avoided even being close to him. It was then that the husband realized his wife had translated the common term for Cat operator into German and honestly believed Ginter was killing and skinning cats for a living. He set her straight on the way home and the woman said she had learned another colloquialism she could not have picked up in the English classes she took every week. Ginter never knew how much he had upset the German woman.

Bob Harkins, a well-known broadcaster and local historian in northern British Columbia saw another face of Ginter's multi-faceted personality. He had interviewed Ginter at the CJCI radio station which was then located at the top of the city's Inn of the North hotel. The two men retired to the coffee-shop. The cafe was empty except for themselves and a young couple with a small child. The baby was fascinated by Ginter's bushy beard and it made cooing noises to convey his pleasure. Ginter turned around and entertained the child. He made funny faces; he made funny noises and enjoyed himself as much as the toddler. Harkins said the parents were beaming with pride that Ginter spent considerable time with the child.

"As we were the only ones in the coffee-shop, it was not a grandstand-play, Ginter genuinely had fun and so did the kid. Had I not seen this, I would not have believed it," Harkins said.

At one point the City of Prince George became one of Ginter's targets. He claimed he was being treated unfairly over his contribution of land for a school in a new subdivision. Ginter and his land manager Bob Naismith accused the city of forcing Ginter to put up most of the public lands needed in the Pinecone Subdivision for the school and parks. Ginter owned fifty-two acres in the area and had to put up seventeen acres for the public good. Ginter could not help attacking the city's mayor, Harold Moffat, whose family business Northern Hardware and Furniture Company Limited, also owned land in the area. Ginter accused Moffat and other land owners of not putting up their fair shares. Moffat, like Ginter, was not a man to take things lying down. "We paid compensation for the land," the mayor said, "the equivalent of contributing land."

City Manager Chester Jeffrey had told Ginter that he would be paid money for the unequal appropriation of his land. Land owners could pay cash to the city instead of donating land for their share of public land allowances required under the subdivision agreement. The Moffats had chosen to pay cash; Ginter had chosen to donate land, Jeffrey said. He would be paid for any land in excess of his share.

Ginter was not satisfied because he questioned why he should be paid for undeveloped land while others gave the cash value of undeveloped land while keeping the land for development. Those who paid cash got to develop the land and then sell it at a profit. Those who donated land didn't get the chance to develop and sell at a profit. It was unfair, Ginter said. Jeffrey explained that settlement of the problem was a matter for negotiations and the raw land price meant the price of the land after development costs had been subtracted. At the time the net price was $6,000 an acre.

Ginter was also asked for land by the city which wanted to build the Foothills Boulevard overpass and intersection. The city wanted twelve acres owned by Ginter for this project. Ginter protested it was too much. However, the city needed the property because it would cost an additional $150,000 to $200,000 if the city accepted the alternative proposal of not using Ginter's land but rerouting the four-lane highway. An offer to swap lands with the city was not popular with city council and at least one alderman said a cash settlement was the only acceptable solution.

Ginter had always enjoyed a drink, as he saw it as a good public relations gesture when he drank his own products, which were of top quality. Ben said if he drank his own beer and was seen to drink it, others would drink it. Ginter often saw himself as an example of what a willing and hard-working man could achieve in

Canada, and he was convinced others saw him in a similar light. Ben also developed a taste for scotch. Lack of exercise, irregular eating habits, and long working hours combined with beer and scotch let him reach a weight of nearly two hundred and fifty pounds. Ginter could hold his liquor well; nobody ever saw him not in control of himself after a bout with drink.

10

WHAT DID FASCINATE THE LOCALS was the home Ginter had
built in 1962 on the outskirts of Prince George. Few had ever been
inside, but all were curious. Ginter used the house as a show piece.
He entertained lavishly and always said he hoped that one day the
building would serve as a club house or a meeting place for
important conferences. Ben had thought about building a home
appropriate to his success. The family had been living in a small
bungalow in downtown Prince George, and Ginter had long
dreamed of living in a more secluded area where he could raise
horses and cattle. He found the ideal place on the side of
Cranbrook Hill on the west side of Prince George. The home site
was about halfway up the hill and provided a full view over the
city all the way to Tabor Mountain to the east.

He spoke with architects and builders but did not get the
answers he wanted. So he designed it himself. It would eventually
measure 7,800 square feet including a forty-foot indoor swimming pool covered by a plastic bubble. It was a one-story building
with an all-glass front overlooking the city. Massive redwood
beams which Ginter had personally selected in California carried
the roof. A huge stone fireplace, open to face both sides of the

large L-shaped living room, was a prominent feature. Stone covered walls and a stone floor evoked the appearance of an old style English manor house with a touch of the Canadian West. The polished flagstone floor carried hidden spring-fed water pipes through which hot or cold water was piped, depending on the season. The spring was located behind the house and supplied all water used by the household. Ben was very proud of this system that he designed after the architects told him it could not be done.

A hallway led off to one side of the main room, and its ceiling became the target of much conversation and gossip. Ginter had brought in some Japanese artists who pressed huge butterflies, leaves, and flowers into acrylic. They used the resulting transparent sheets as light fixture covers in the hallway, designed to resemble a passageway of a railway car. Ben loved railways. Doors along the hallway led off to bedrooms and bathrooms, all with heated floors. In the master bedroom the bed was built into a corner. The ensuite featured a sunken bathtub.

A wet bar, partially covered with calf-skins, was located conveniently off the living room. Matching furniture was placed around the room. French sliding doors led on to a patio which ran the length of the building terraced above a paved driveway, which was lined with birch trees. A barbecue, large enough to roast a whole steer, flanked the terrace.

Pasture land sloped down to a ranch house and corrals. This land was the 175-acre ranch which Ginter called Green Valley Ranch. Here he raised his prize Arabian horses and Hereford cattle. This home property comprised some twenty acres and was surrounded by evergreens. Behind the housing complex, Cranbrook Hill provided a backdrop. Built into this background

Front view of Prince George's most elaborate home in late fall. Ben built this home in 1962 on Cranbrook Hill.

The huge fireplace, open on two sides, dominated the open-beamed living room and heated the family dining room.

Butterflies and leaves are preserved in the lit ceiling of the main hallway leading to the bedrooms. The hallway was built to resemble a railway sleeper car. The floor was heated by hot water.

hill was the swimming pool connected by glass doors to the living room. The swimming pool hall featured a recycling waterfall in one corner. Ginter had plans to enlarge the house even more by adding multi-storied living quarters to its rear.

The woods around the property ensured Ginter complete privacy, and few people even knew the place existed. The paved driveway ended at the edge of the property, and guests had to drive on a gravel road for a few hundred yards after leaving city streets until they entered the Ginter complex. A gate made sure uninvited guests stayed out. It was an estate designed to impress and those who saw it for the first time could not help but be impressed. It was built to give the former bulldozer operator a

James and Shane are reading in Dad's study. A picture of a smiling Ben watches from the wall.

place in Prince George society that had openly snubbed him. It was interesting, Ginter said, to see how people acted when they received an invitation from him.

"Most of them fawned," he said disgustedly.

It was true that many people who sneered at Ginter in private or to their friends or even ridiculed him and his tastes in public became quite subservient in his presence. Ginter noticed the change in behaviour. It amused and disgusted him at the same time. Thus, he often treated these people with scorn. Those who he considered to be his friends, Ginter treated royally at his home. Receiving an invitation to attend a function at the "Ginter Place" was almost like being knighted, one reporter wrote.

Calf-hide decorated the bar at the Ginter house, adding a western touch, which Ben favoured.

Ben's indoor pool was the only one in Prince George at the time.

On occasions Ginter liked to invite members of the media to the house or to the brewery. For some years the brewery had held open house for the media each Friday and on occasions Ginter would put in an appearance. He would talk with anyone and always seemed to be interested in what was going on in town. He was also remarkably well informed on local events.

The Citizen staff mostly consisted of young and single people who liked to party. Eugene Zarek, Ben's brew-master, could always be relied upon to contribute some beer to these parties. On one weekend one of Ginter's younger employees came to a party as a date of one of the reporters.

The party lasted quite a while. On Monday morning when the young woman had to go to work, she was still suffering somewhat from the festivities. Ginter called and asked me to come and see him at his office. He looked very serious and said he understood one of his employees had been our staff's guest and still was not really fit to work. He did not like that, he said, and added that he also understood that some of the beer that been flowing so freely had been contributed by his brewery. I was mentally mourning the loss of our free beer when Ginter suddenly said, "How come I am never invited?" I explained that we did not think it appropriate to ask a man of his stature to party with us and added that there would be a party on the following weekend at the same place. Ginter showed up for the party in a pick-up truck loaded with beer. He really seemed to have a good time. I know we did.

On another occasion Ginter called me on a Friday afternoon after work when *The Citizen* staff was relaxing from the week's strain at the Inn of the North. He wanted to see me at once. When I told him I was off work and enjoying a beer, he asked if I was paying for the beer. "You come over now and you won't have to pay for your beer," he told me. I asked him if he would mind if I brought my colleagues along. He said that was fine. We had a swim in his pool and enjoyed that Friday until early Saturday. Ginter, it seemed, just wanted some company.

Ben Ginter sometimes entertained the rich or famous at his place without anyone in Prince George being aware. He would fly his guests in with his own aircraft and then have loyal employees drive them to the house. He knew he could trust the employees never to talk about his guests. Ginter liked to keep his private life private. Ben would inform Grace of the guests at the last possible moment, but he expected her to provide the food and entertainment to make his guests welcome. She said that Ben would bring any number of people home at any time. The one or two reporters he sometimes included in his functions could be relied on to keep the identities of his guests secret. When road construction was in full bloom in British Columbia, and Ginter had earned his place as the prime contractor, he used to call Highways Minister Phil Gaglardi to discuss upcoming contracts. Even Gaglardi made his pilgrimage to the house on the hill in Prince George.

After Ginter's holdings were placed in receivership he tried to sell the house without success and it became part of his estate after he died. A new owner, Cliff Turner, tried to turn it into a men's club and then a restaurant, but could not put it on a profitable base. He put it up for auction and it sold for $187,000, a far cry from Ginter's asking price of some $400,000. When yet the next owner was unable to pay the mortgage, the house reverted to the bank.

As the city expanded the privacy was destroyed by encroaching subdivisions. The ranch house, barn and paddocks disappeared as did most of the tree belt. The view from the hill was marred by the multicoloured roofs of the single family dwellings spreading out below. A road to provide access to the new University of Northern British Columbia is being built behind the house and plans for the completion of Foothills Boulevard call for cutting through the meadows in front of the Ginter property. These measures provide the last blow to what once was one of Prince George's best pieces of real estate. The area has deteriorated over the years to such an extent that today, teenagers use the green meadows in front of the estate as a sort of 'lover's lane' and the meadows even figured prominently as the scene of a rape case.

11

BEN INADVERTENTLY GOT INTO THE BUSINESS that was to make him notorious. In 1962 Ben Ginter was looking for a new yard in Prince George to store and to repair his heavy construction machinery. The yard on First Avenue was no longer large enough to hold his ever-increasing fleet. At the same time, he had to store idle equipment, as road construction had slowed down somewhat from the heady days of the 1950s. It was not easy to locate a suitable site in the city which, although it had grown along with the rest of the province, was still a small town. The site needed proper buildings, water, power and accessibility. Ginter's people were looking all over the area and finally found what they were looking for on the banks of the Nechako River. The plant of the Cariboo Brewing Company Ltd. had been sitting idle since it had been placed in receivership. It had been built in 1957 at a cost of $850,000 but the company could not make a profit and the Canadian Imperial Bank of Commerce (CIBC) took it over when operations closed and appointed Harold Sigurdson as receiver.

While private entrepreneurs built the brewery, Labatt's bought it in an effort to kill all competition from independent brewers in British Columbia. Many in Prince George, if not most, believed that the beer produced under the national label was of low quality. Furthermore, they argued that producing low quality beer was deliberate, so the national company could ultimately shut down the operation when sales became too low.

Ginter took one look at the plant and declared it suitable for a new construction yard. He paid $150,000 for the land and the buildings. He certainly had no intentions to enter into the brewing business. The decision to purchase the property changed Ginter's history, made him a nationally-known personality, and eventually spawned his dream of empire. It also became the source of his future problems.

The site was a mess. Vandals had broken into the building earlier to damage and destroy machinery, windows, pipes, and just about everything they could reach. Time had done the rest; the place was filthy. Paint was peeling, the roof was leaking, and birds were nesting inside. Light fixtures and wiring were in disrepair if not pulled off the walls and ceilings. However, the buildings were still filled with brewing equipment including a huge copper brewing kettle made in Chicago, dating back to 1912. The rest of the machinery was rusting.

Ginter planned to throw out everything he could not use or sell. Since selling the machinery called for a major clean-up, he set his crews to work at once. Word of the purchase and the plans to turn the former brewery into a construction yard spread through Prince George. Mayor Garvin Dezell; some businessmen; and, most importantly, B.C. Lands, Forest and Water Resources Minister Ray Williston felt there already were too many construction yards around the city. They also felt a functioning brewery would be a good thing for Prince George. Williston was the first to try to persuade Ginter that there was value in having a producing brewery in the North-central Interior of the province.

Dezell, himself the owner of a construction company, joined Williston's approach to Ginter and asked that he restore the brewery to its original use. There was always a market for beer, he told Ginter. The town was growing and a new brewing venture would not falter for a lack of customers. The local hotels supported the mayor. It pleased Ginter that he had been asked, but he was reluctant to move into a business he knew nothing about. Williston and Dezell put pressure on Ginter by asking what did he have to lose in giving it a try. Ginter agreed to lay out some $250,000 to buy the brewing business.

"This is all I am going to venture; the business either makes it or not, but I'll not risk more money on it," Ginter told Williston. He figured this was going to appease Williston and the mayor while at the same time he could afford to invest that amount. Should he lose it, Ginter said, he could always write it off on his taxes. The minister quietly helped to arrange licence through Attorney-General Robert Bonner. When word of Ginter's decision became public knowledge, Williston and Dezell unwittingly acquired help in their persuasive efforts from the most unlikely quarter, the national breweries.

Ginter received a call from one of the major breweries in Vancouver with a plea for help. He was told the brew kettle at the Vancouver plant had so severely broken down that it had to be replaced. The nearest available one was in Ginter's newly acquired plant in Prince George. The caller said his company was willing to pay anything Ginter asked. When Ginter held out, he was offered the astonishing amount of $150,000 for the kettle, the

A crane raises the new Ben's colours at the refurbished brewery, signalling the start of Ben's Tartan empire.

price Ginter paid for the whole former brewery complex. This made him sit up and listen.

If a national brewer were willing to pay as much just for one piece of equipment as he had paid for the plant, there had to be an ulterior motive. Ginter's business sense told him he was not being told the truth. He became certain he was offered that much for the kettle just to keep him from entering the brewing field. He was also convinced that there must be money to be made if a national company was willing to offer that amount just to keep him out. And if there was a profit in it, why shouldn't he make it? Ginter decided right then to become a beer baron. He admitted he knew nothing about making beer, but then Ginter always was a fast learner.

Tartan Brewing, one of Prince George's major employers, proudly signalling the start of Ben's Tartan empire.

The piece of equipment which sparked Ben's money-making instincts met an ignominious end. The 5,200 gallon copper brew kettle was used until 1978 when it was replaced by a larger more modern stainless steel one. By then Ginter had lost the brewery, and the new owners first wanted to place the old kettle on the roof of the building as a landmark. In the end it was sold for scrap and brought $5,000, a far cry from what Ginter had been offered.

Once he had decided to operate full steam ahead, Ginter put together a team headed by Eugene Zarek, an Austrian-born brewmaster who had worked in Regina, Saskatchewan for thirty years. Zarek hired a crew to train because there were few people around Prince George who knew much about beer brewing and still less how to operate a brewery. Zarek moved to Prince George. Only two months after Ginter had acquired the brewery, beer started

Production manager Henry Binder inspects the carton as the first Tartan is readied for market.

to flow from the restored plant. Ginter called his new possession Tartan Industries Limited because he liked tartans. He liked them so much, in fact, that he put them on the labels of his new products. The interior and offices of the brewery were also decorated with tartans. He donated tartans to the Prince George branch of the Royal Canadian Legion for what was — and still is — called the Tartan Room.

Market studies and the failure of the Cariboo brewing venture had taught Ginter that he needed a new strategy to break into the northern provincial beer market. He needed something to give him an edge over his competitors. Subsequently he named his brands of beer "Hi Life," "Paaps," and "Budd," borrowing names freely from popular American brands, albeit spelling them differently. American beer was not sold in British Columbia in those days, but every Canadian who had ever travelled in the United States or had watched American TV, was familiar with or at least had heard of these brands. Ginter hoped the name association would help him sell his Prince George brew.

It did, but it was mainly curiosity which drew beer drinkers to the new brands. American breweries were unhappy about Ginter's choices and demanded he change the names of his brands. It would take a court order to force Ginter to comply. Meanwhile, there was a big celebration when the first bottled Prince George brew hit the liquor stores, but Ginter's dream of turning instant beer baron overnight did not materialize.

Drinking beer in Canada was — and in some places still is — a rather primitive ritual. All drinking in public had to be done in hotels in special places commonly called beer parlours. In B.C. at this time laws mandated segregated beer parlours, which meant men were drinking on one side of a wall or partition, while women sat alone on the other side. Sometimes they were in separate halls or rooms. Men accompanied by women were allowed to enter the women's side of the establishments. It is still hard to find a rationale for this, but it was widely assumed that unaccompanied men would offend female customers with their rough language, should they be sitting close together in the same room.

It was also the custom to serve two beers per customer at one time. The rules said, however, there could be no more than double the number of glasses on the table than there were people sitting there. Patrons were not allowed to stand up and drink; neither were they allowed to carry their brew from one table to another, should they decide to move. Singing and the playing of instruments was not allowed, although each beer parlour usually had a juke box. It was a rather archaic system designed to sell as much beer in the shortest possible time. No thought was given to the enjoyment of the drinkers. Drinking beer seemed to have been regarded as a sinful deed, best hidden from the public view. For example, if a hotel beer parlour had windows, they were painted over in black, making it impossible for the innocent passers-by to look in and be corrupted. Following the British tradition, at an earlier time, parlours even closed in the late afternoon until after supper time ostensibly to assure that patrons would go home for supper but, hopefully, return later.

Hotels had a monopoly on beer sales, but were subject to the rules set by the British Columbia Liquor Control Board in Victoria. One of the rules was that a hotel had to apply for the right to sell a certain brand of beer, and if a hotel owner wanted to change brands, he had to apply for the right to change. Hotels were allowed to change brands once a year.

When Ginter started to market his draught beer in Prince George he found that all hotels were, of course, already being served by the Big Three in Canadian brewing: Molson, Labatt's, and Carling-O'Keefe. The town, like the rest of the province, was sewn up because there was no other beer on the market. Ginter started to lobby hotel owners to apply for a change. He hoped some would be willing to try and give his beer a chance. Publicly he started to decry the monopolies of the Big Three and the unfairness of government in not changing the rules. The seeds of a long drawn-out fight were sown.

One hotel in Prince George took a chance on Ginter's beer, applied for a change in brands, and got it. This hotel, the Canada Hotel, was located in the rougher part of town on the corner of

Second Avenue and George Street, one block from the city's most notorious intersection of Third and George. This corner was the image the rest of the country had of Prince George. Who could forget the news photo showing a man swinging by his arms from the sign of the McDonald Hotel, or "Mac" as it was affectionately known, located right at the intersection? While a huge crowd cheered him on, RCMP officers tried to get him down. The photo had been splashed on the front pages of newspapers across the country. The area attracted local hosts who took their guests slumming in the area, curious about the clientele of both the Mac and the Canada Hotel. A reveller could find just about anything he wished in this area of town, be it booze, drugs, or sex.

Drinking was Prince George's favourite pastime. The city had the highest per capita consumption of beer in the province. Since British Columbia had the highest beer consumption of all the provinces, it stood to reason that Prince George was the beer drinking capital of the nation. Each morning in provincial court, drunks were paraded before the judge after spending the night — or at least part of the night — in the city jail's drunk tank. Police picked up public drunks and just let them sleep it off on the bare cell floor. While this may appear to be a crude way of handling drunks, police saved the lives of quite a few imbibers, especially in the winter when temperatures dropped to as low as -40 degrees. Drunks were often found in snowdrifts, and had police not picked them up, they would have frozen to death during the night.

In those days being drunk in a public place was an offence, and Judge George O. Stewart, who was to become the longest serving provincial court judge in British Columbia, would get to know most of his customers by name because of their repeat appearances.

The rowdiness which took place on the corner of Third Avenue and George Street would spill over along George Street and after-hours parties in what were called "booze cans" — illegal bootlegging establishments — contributed to the city's reputation of "the wildest place in B.C."

These illegal booze outlets, to some extent, were the result of the restrictive liquor laws of British Columbia. While some people frequented these establishments on any day during the week, they were especially busy during the weekends. Legal drinking places were required to shut off the supply on Saturday night at 11:30 p.m. sharp, and the beer parlours had to be vacated half an hour later. Most of the weekend drinkers had spent the week in the bush and were ready to live it up. They would just be ready to get going at the time the hotels closed their beer parlours. Now they found themselves on the street. Someone always knew the location of a "booze can" and these places did land office business. Police were aware of these illegal places and would raid as often as manpower allowed. They closed the operation down; the court fined the operators who then would be back in business at a different location, often on the same day.

On a dare, I once accompanied Ben Ginter to a booze can. He had told me he had never been to one and was curious. As court reporter for *The Citizen*, I knew the locations of several of these establishments. The one I chose was located on the road to one of the pulp mills, and it was commonly known as "Fuzzies." It was a three-bedroom stucco house, and, from the outside, was like hundreds of others in the city. Inside, however, the similarity ended. The only furniture was couches placed along the walls. There was only one table and a few chairs in the kitchen. The kitchen counter served as the bar. A burly fellow poured drinks from bottles, all equipped with measuring spouts. He handed you a drink, and you handed over 75 cents, regardless what kind of drink you ordered. Mix was free as long as it was the orange juice, found in the large pitchers on the tables and counters. Bottled mix cost a quarter. Ashtrays were placed strategically around the rooms. When we arrived, I knocked at the door and, like in an old gangster movie, a spy hole opened. We were asked who we were looking for. "Fuzzies," I said and the door was opened.

There was silence as Ginter walked in with me, as he was instantly recognized. Ginter nodded to the doorkeeper but otherwise ignored the clientele, many of whom I had often seen around the courts. We walked into the kitchen and Ginter ordered two drinks. Scotch for himself and rye for me. He looked around silently, his face without expression. The place was crowded, and when Ginter pushed through to the bar, a few people greeted him, but most were just staring and whispering to their companions.

"Think they got beer?" he asked. I knew what was coming: Ginter was looking for his own brands at a bootlegger. We asked for beer, and the bartender pulled a few bottles from the fridge behind him. I just knew: Ben was going to complain because the label showed the brew was a national brand. Before the bartender uncapped the brew, Ginter said he had changed his mind and asked for another scotch. I also passed on the beer. We did not stay long, and later in the car, Ginter said in a dead voice, "They must be making pretty good money." I thought it was a good idea we left early because police raided these places frequently, and Ginter could do without the resulting publicity, should he be found in a booze can. We never mentioned that evening again.

The Mac beer parlour was always filled with noisy crowds, and those who could not find a seat spilled over into the Canada Hotel, owned by Bill Cutt at that time. He had taken a chance in becoming the only public draught beer outlet Ginter would ever have in all his years in the beer business. One or two Royal Canadian Legion posts also carried his draught, but they were clubs, not public houses.

Ginter's bottled beer fared somewhat better. It was placed in the government-run liquor stores throughout the province and, at first, sales were brisk because people were eager to try something new. After curiosity waned, sales stagnated. Because Ginter did not believe that people would not buy his beer, he blamed the liquor stores, saying his brands were placed in difficult-to-find locations. He demanded that more prominent displays be made. He also accused the liquor board of pushing the national brands in its stores. He went as far as suggesting there was a conspiracy between the liquor board, individual store managers, and the big breweries.

12

It was the first time he subscribed to a conspiracy theory in saying the Big Three breweries would employ any method to get him out of the business because they feared for their monopoly position throughout Canada. He would also speak to all reporters who would listen, trying to convince them that Tartan beer was being discriminated against. No doubt, Ginter's beer was different from the common brands of beer sold in Canada. Eugene Zarek, an Old World gentleman, liked to brew a more European beer rather than the Canadian lager or pilsner. Europeans like their brew with a bit of a bitter flavour, while Canadians like theirs sweeter without a bitter aftertaste. Many European immigrants bought nothing but Ginter's beer after they discovered the taste, saying it reminded them of real beer instead of the limp-wristed, shallow taste of North American brews. Overall, these immigrants who had tasted American beers preferred any beer brewed in Canada.

Ginter could not be convinced that he wasn't being discriminated against; he insisted everyone was against him and his beer. Spreading rumours had it that Ginter's beer was brewed with water from the Nechako River which flows right by the brewery.

Brewmaster Zarek conducts a quality check on beer as a visitor looks on.

People said Ginter was not telling the truth when he claimed his brew was made with spring water. However, he was speaking the truth because beneath the brewery site are aquifers or underground springs with the purest of waters. Ginter had the water tested by top laboratories and the results were that Tartan spring water was as good as any of the world famous springs. He distributed the laboratory results to the press. He thought of printing them on his beer boxes, an action which apparently was against liquor board rules. Ginter's constant complaints to the liquor board and the attorney-general soon earned him the reputation of being querulous and quarrelsome. Ginter denied he was either, but did not change his methods of operations to forestall his critics.

Wherever Ginter's beer was sold, either in bottles or as draught, problems followed. Beer salesmen for the national breweries would bring friends or some thirsty, but out-of-money fellows whom they met in the streets into a pub and then buy them a Ginter beer. As soon as these mercenaries would take a swig, they would spit it out and loudly complain about the "pig swill" they had been sold. The "bought" drinkers had been well coached. They would demand a "good" beer.

The salesmen would then order the brands they represented. After the first sip the drinkers would praise the brew highly and loudly. When the curiosity of the rest of the customers was aroused, the salesmen would buy a round for everyone. It was a successful, if dirty, tactic.

One early incident helped his opponents claim his beer would cause stomach problems and was green, that is, not aged well enough before being sold. His enemies claimed Ginter was in such a hurry to get his product on the market he would not let it age properly, a charge Ginter vehemently denied. The brewery admitted that one early batch had turned out bad for some reason and some drinkers reported diarrhoea after drinking a bottle or two. Many beer lovers, however, believed the rumours and never again bought a Ginter product.

Ginter pointed out that even the most established brewery was sometimes plagued by inexplicable product errors. His competitors made the most of the green beer incident, forever establishing the rumour that all Ginter beer was green. This was, of course, contrary to what was actually happening. Ginter made sure that only top quality beer would leave the brewery in order to counter the rumours. Whatever he did, his beer was not selling well at all.

These skirmishes dragged on for years and Ginter began looking for new advantages. He found one when he introduced the beer can in 1966. It had been attempted earlier on a small scale but British Columbians had not been ready to drink beer from a metal container, claiming however incorrectly that there was a metallic taste to it. The public was finally ready, in 1966. Ginter had quietly installed a canning line at the brewery, had designed a red and yellow can with tartans, and named this new product "PILcan." It was an instant hit with consumers who liked the smaller packaging, the handy cans, and taste of the beer.

The Big Three were just as quick in disliking it. Harley Deeks, a highly-placed executive in Molson's was in Prince George a few weeks after Ginter had introduced PILcan. Deeks dismissed the canned beer as a gimmick and a flash in the pan, but said all other brewers would market canned beer in British Columbia should Ginter's market share ever reach four per cent. By the time the nationals got around to selling their beer in cans, Ginter had already exceeded the four per cent share of the market. For a while Ginter was doing well and he faced no major problems. Then the competition hit back.

Carling Breweries (BC) Limited sued Ginter for the use of the name PILcan, saying Pil was their registered trade name and that Ginter's use of it infringed on their trademark. Angry, Ginter channelled his considerable energy into a renewed fight with the Big Three. It did not matter to him which of the three was involved; he considered them all his mortal enemies sworn to drive him from the business. By then Ginter had gained nearly seven per cent of the beer market in British Columbia with his cans, and the Big Three had finally got around to marketing their own canned beer two years later. Tartan Brewery then brought another invention to the industry: pull-tabs for the cans and a ring-pull for bottles eliminating the need for a can or bottle opener.

Then came a shock for the Prince George brewery. The courts ordered Ginter to pull all PILcan beer from the shelves of the liquor stores and turn over all cartons, cans and labels bearing the name PILcan to Carling's for destruction. Ginter was in no hurry to comply. The ordered withdrawal of the brand was to be in effect until the trademark dispute was settled. It was a major setback for Ginter. It was not the only one.

When the Big Three started to sell canned beer in British Columbia, they asked the liquor board to be allowed to add their premium to the price of the beer, making it twenty cents a dozen more expensive than bottled beer. This was their usual practice although Ginter saw no reason for it as he had been charging bottle price for canned beer all along and had been making money. He did not join the petition for a price increase. The board ordered all canned beer to be included in the price increase to maintain the usual price conformity that the board demanded from all brewers throughout the province.

Ginter immediately launched a protest. There was no economic need for the increase. He told the press that consumers would save about $125,000 a year by buying his beer at the old price, based on estimated sales for 1969. The liquor control board would have none of this. Ginter was ordered to comply or lose his licence to make beer in the province. "They explained to me that the rules called for price conformity and said it did not matter that my costs have not increased and that I did not need this hike," Ginter said. Always thinking, Ginter came up with a way to get around the rule. He had his employees tape a dime to each dozen pack of cans made by his plant, thereby returning the increase to the buyer.

Victoria was furious and issued an immediate cease and desist order. Ginter stopped returning the dimes to his customers but complained loudly about the unfairness of it all. Now came the clincher to this ridiculous episode. While the other beer producers shared in the profits from the price increase, Ginter did not. The liquor control board informed him that, since he had not applied for the increase, he was not entitled to the profits from it. It made no sense, but there it was; Ginter was stymied, but unbeaten. He was not about to let those Victoria bureaucrats threaten him as if he was a nobody. "I had not asked for the price hike because I did not need it. But they ordered me to do it and now they don't want me to have the extra profits the others share. Their attitude is, 'I didn't ask so why should I get it?'" he said.

The attorney-general's ministry had to intervene to get Ben his share. This ministry agreed it did not matter whether Ginter had asked for the increase or had resisted it; the extra money had been earned from the sale of his products. Thus, he was entitled to his share of the price boost. Ginter then unilaterally increased the refund on a dozen of cans to ten cents and then raised it to twenty-five cents; the liquor board could not touch him. Ben had beaten city hall for once . . . .

All of these manoeuvres did not help when he was forced to

remove PILcan from the shelves, pending the court decision as to whether the word "Pil" could be copyrighted in Canada.

"Pil is short for Pilsner, a specific type of beer brewed first in the city of Pilsen in Czechoslovakia; it is recognized as such all around the world," Ginter said. The Exchequer Court of Canada, in a curious twist of events, gave Ginter the right to sell PILcan in Manitoba, the Yukon, and Northwest Territories as well as in Alaska, but not in British Columbia. Ginter was also going to court to ask for permission to sell in Alberta. By this time he owned breweries in both Alberta and Manitoba, which would supply the beer for the court-permitted sale. This odd situation happened because until 1992, Canada's inter-provincial trade agreements stipulated that beer could be sold only in the province where the producer had a brewery. Special permission had to be granted by governments to sell beer from other provinces.

The absence of PILcan in British Columbia hurt, and Ginter again frantically looked for a solution. He found not only one but two. He dropped the PILcan label in favour of calling his beer "Uncle Ben's." Here he was on safe ground as there was not even one similar sounding beer brand on the market. It is not known whether the makers of Uncle Ben's Rice ever raised any objections. That was Solution Number One. Next he applied for a licence to brew a beer with ten per cent alcohol content. Until this point, Canadian beer usually had had an alcohol content of between four and five per cent. He also applied to the federal department of health which ruled on questions involving food. Beer is classified as a food, and Ben wanted permission to call his new brand "Uncle Ben's Malt Liquor." All beer in Canada is defined by law as malt liquor, but the name is normally applied now to beer containing more than five per cent alcohol.

Eugene Zarek had started to work on the problem of coming up with a new product for Ginter. He was looking for a stronger beer with an acceptable taste. Zarek had a laboratory right next to his brew-master's office in the brew-house of the plant. Here he experimented mixing various concoctions of hops, malt, flavours, and spirits over a period of time, but he was without success. As soon as the alcohol level rose to above eight per cent, the brew took on too strong an alcohol taste, or it would taste too strongly of malt. The brew-master was sure such beer would never sell in British Columbia. He tried to mix scotch, gin, or rye with the hops and malt and eventually hit on using vodka in his mixtures. He found what he wanted, a beer that tasted good without any of the flavours dominating. From the formula he devised, he was able to reverse the working process and have the beer create its own additional alcohol naturally, eliminating the experimental vodka. Zarek believed he had found a winner and Ginter agreed.

On May 15, 1969 the first Uncle Ben's Malt Liquor was bottled in Prince George and shipments left the brewery the same day to liquor store warehouses across the province. The first customers in Prince George could hardly believe their eyes.

Finally the masses could see Uncle Ben. On the label, Ben looked at them sporting a beard, while sitting in front of a waterfall. The picture was surrounded by tartans. But, as most people in Prince George knew, Ben was clean-shaven. Ginter had not had time to grow one for the label photo: he was wearing a fake. He later grew his own foliage, explaining he had always wanted to grow a beard, but had given up after a few days because the new growth would itch too much. This time it was going to be different because it would promote his beer.

Ginter was a great promoter. He attended many small-town rodeos and fairs where there usually was a beer garden. He would sit with the locals and talk, buying the occasional round and be one of the boys. This happened, however, at events where his beer was sold exclusively. In time, Ginter became known as "Uncle Ben," a role he relished. Although I got along well with Ginter as reporter for *The Prince George Citizen*, I was not impressed by the new label. The day I saw him grinning at me from a beer bottle, I wrote in my column:

> "Ginter's picture on the label of his new brand of beer is about as popular in Prince George as Hitler's in Jerusalem."

Ginter did not like my remarks, but took it in good spirits because he felt he had a winning product. The column was an accurate reflection of feelings many Prince George residents harboured about Ben Ginter. Because he was wealthy and there-fore an object of envy, many people saw him as nothing but a tycoon out for himself. Ginter liked his countenance on the label, and he was willing to risk a good deal of money to keep it before the public. About then, a California convenience store chain became interested in selling his beer. Ginter sent a negotiation team to San Francisco and they struck a deal. However, one item the Californians did not like was Ginter's picture on the label. They wanted a label showing clear, cool northern waters indicat-ing the properties of this wild water to quench a California thirst. Head negotiator, Joe Rinaldi, told the Americans he would get

Ginter's agreement for a new label. He flew back to Vancouver to report to Ginter on the negotiations. Ginter was pleased.

"There's just one other thing we have to clear up," Rinaldi told Ginter. Then he explained the objections the Californians had to Ginter's label. Ginter listened and then waved his hand.

"Well, that settles that, the label stays," Ginter said, killing a most lucrative contract which would have opened the vast American beer market because of his own vanity. Rinaldi said you could not have Ben's product without buying Ben's picture; Ginter's ego was part of any deal.

The dislike, locally and province-wide, of the new label translated into slumping beer sales. At this point Ginter did not really care. Prince George, after all, was only a small place which had become his headquarters by chance. He had bigger things in mind. Ginter was dreaming of expanding eastward. Since trade barriers demanded that most of the beer sold in any given province had to be produced there, brewers had to set up plants in whichever province they wanted to sell their products.

13

A STRIKE HAD SHUT DOWN all but his brewery in British Columbia. Since Uncle Ben's was the only beer available, sales were going great and were even picking up in Prince George. Ginter's brewery workers belonged to the same union as those on strike, but their contract had a different expiration day, and they were therefore not involved. Uncle Ben's was being churned out while the brew-houses of the national beer makers sat idle. As beer supplies began to dwindle, hotel owners who, prior to the strike, would not look at Ginter's beer, flooded him with requests for the valuable suds. All but one of the province's beer parlours were forced to shut down. The sole operating one was the Canada Hotel in Prince George, Ginter's only draught outlet. This hotel did such good business that owner Bill Cutt remodelled his beer parlour after the strike ended. It became the nicest looking watering hole in the province, and set a standard for remodelling the generally depressing beer parlours, turning them into more cheerful places.

As the brewery operated around the clock, Ginter offered to supply draught beer to others, but the liquor control board would not change its regulation. If a hotel changed to Ginter's beer, it would have to stay with it until the owners were allowed to make their once-a-year brand change. Many hotels were wary of this obligation, as they worried that Ginter would not be able to produce enough beer to supply them in normal times. Some did take the chance because the lack of income from the beer parlours threatened their hotels' existence. While Ginter was able to pick up a few new accounts, he lost most of them again as soon as these hotels could legally change back to a different supplier.

At the Canada Hotel, business was booming and the scene was beyond description. Patrons were packed in like sardines in a can, and waiters dumped large numbers of glasses on each table. It did not matter how many glasses the customers ordered; their table would be filled with whatever the waiter had on his tray. If a customer's beer ran low, the waiter automatically dumped another load and collected his money. If the customer did not want more, he was asked to leave immediately because there were others waiting to take his place. Drunks were grabbed and ejected through the swinging doors without much ado. Government regulations said patrons had to be seated when served. At the Canada Hotel the number of drinkers outstripped the seating capacity, but beer drinkers proved to be inventive. Quite a few brought metal or wooden buckets along, turned them upside down and created their own seats. The waiters did not object. These people were sitting and that was all that mattered.

Ginter was still not happy. He demanded that normal liquor board rules about changing brands be suspended for the duration of the strike to allow him to supply anyone who asked for his beer. The board was not about to do so.

"Here I am sitting on all that beer and am not allowed to sell most of it. That is crass discrimination," he thundered. He accused the board of being in bed with the Big Three and of safeguarding their monopoly status during the strike because the board did not suspend the normal rules in an abnormal time. Ginter vowed to fight on. He maintained the big breweries were keeping relentless pressure on him because they knew that should he successfully penetrate their sales areas in other provinces, he would set a precedent that could result in other companies trying to do the same, cutting into the Big Three's profits. His pleas for under-standing fell on deaf ears.

The strike ended with a new agreement, but Ginter managed to keep his union contract separate from the others, holding on to the different expiration date. Now his sales slipped back to pre-strike days, and Ginter pondered the lack of loyalty among beer drinkers. Later Ben Ginter would say the beer industry was the most "crude, most discriminatory and the dirtiest business" in Canada. "I'd like to switch to pulp and paper because it is clean compared with the beer industry," he once said. He claimed there was more graft, more laws broken in the beer industry than in any other ". . . unless it's in the Mafia."

"I work sixteen hours a day just to stay alive," he said of his battles with the Big Three. The question which always puzzled the public and those close to Ginter was — why did the Big Three expend so much energy to defeat a small independent brewer whose yearly production was but a drop in a bucket compared to that of the national brewers? Former Lands, Forests and Water Resources Minister Ray Williston believes the Big Three were worried about Ginter because he was unpredictable.

"You never knew what Ben would be doing next; he kept his

Brewmaster Eugene Zarek guides a visitor through the brewery. This was taken in front of the copper brewing kettle, for which Ben was offered $150,000, a bribe to keep him out of the brewing business.

competitors off balance," Williston said, adding this unpredictability seemed to unnerve the Big Three into actions which were not necessary and, in hindsight, quite stupid such as their attempt to keep Ginter out of the beer business by trying to buy the brew kettle.

Whatever was wrong with this industry, Ben was not about to get out; instead he changed his tactics. When the provincial government appointed a Royal Commission to probe the liquor industry, Ginter grabbed the chance to promote his ideas. He challenged the commission to call before it former Attorney General Robert Bonner and all liquor board officials as witnesses to the discrimination he claimed he had suffered from the first day he entered the beer business. Ginter submitted a fifty-four page brief, calling for an explanation by Bonner and the board of how they had administered the Liquor Control Act since 1962. He testified he had no problems obtaining a federal licence to brew beer, but when he applied to the provincial government to sell beer, the process turned into a dragged-out affair.

"I had difficulties convincing Mr. Bonner that I could survive the competition," Ginter testified. He had agreed not to sell shares to the public, something he considered a business restriction as he told the commission. By now he was sure that his venture could survive, so he demanded equal treatment from the liquor board and asked that the restriction be lifted. The government granted Ginter permission to market his shares. He lamented the loss of draught accounts he had acquired during the strike because the board had done what it had told him could not be done: it had allowed hotels to switch back to their former brands after the strike was over, even though some were not entitled to do so under the rules. He was joined in his protest by Fort George MLA Ray Williston.

Ginter told the commission that when a customer orders his beer from the liquor board, he must print the word "Tartan" on the order form and a copy of this form was then handed to Pacific Brewers Warehouse, the distributing arm of the Big Three. This, Ginter pointed out, told his competitors how much of his beer was being sold and who bought it. In turn, their salesmen then could call on the outlets and try to convince them to apply for a change to their brands. "This is clearly an unfair trading practice," Ginter testified. He also had constructive ideas for the commission. For instance, he suggested revisions of the liquor act to allow wine and beer to be sold in grocery stores, supermarkets, and other outlets to anyone of legal age. He pointed out that doing so in the United States and other countries had not resulted in any undue proliferation of drunkenness.

His consistent thrusts against all and sundry who he believed stood in the way of free enterprise were designed to keep him in the public eye and to keep his competitors on alert. This hearing revealed just how far Ginter would go to further his interest. At the hearing, the presiding judge confronted him with a certificate which had been issued by Tartan Brewery over the signature of Henry Binder, Ginter's executive. The certificate offered a free turkey, as it had been issued around Thanksgiving. Certificates similar to the one the judge produced at the hearing had been sent to every liquor store manager in British Columbia in clear contravention of liquor regulations. It was a blatant attempt to present government officials with a gift, a completely illegal move. When the judge asked Ginter what he knew about that, Ginter asked who had signed the certificate.

"The signature says Henry Binder," the judge said.

Ginter jumped up, turned to the rear of the hearing, and shouted "Henry, how could you? He did it, Your Honour," pointing at Binder who sat in the back. What he neglected to say was that the idea had come from Ginter himself. He had told Binder to see that the certificates went out over Binder's signature. Ginter was a picture of perfect innocence at the hearing. Years later, Binder would say that only very few certificates had been returned; most had been used.

All of this masked Ginter's real intention which was increased expansion across Canada. He was no longer content to operate only in British Columbia. He wanted to be a national figure. Stunts like the turkey certificate were designed to prevent his competitors from finding out too soon what his plans were. He first moved into Manitoba and Ontario. He choose the city of Cornwall in Ontario for the site of his first brewery outside British Columbia. Winnipeg was his second choice. Alberta and Saskatchewan were next on his list. Amid all this, Ginter announced he wanted to purchase Molson, the old establishment brewery which, among other things, owned the Montreal Canadiens of the National Hockey League. Ginter's plans were ambitious. If Molson could own a hockey team, so could he. Ginter bought 37,000 shares in the Vancouver Canucks.

He grandly announced in 1969 he was putting together a consortium with European backing to gain controlling interest in Molson's enterprises amounting to about $115 million. This offer was only for the majority shares in the brewing operations and did not include the Montreal Canadiens, nor did it include Vilas Industries Limited, a manufacturer of expensive furniture and school equipment which Molson had acquired in 1967. While the public was awed by such grandiose and ambitious plans, the Molson family was not impressed. The majority of shares were held by the family and were not for sale.

The plan was soon dropped, but Ginter got miles of publicity from this ploy. If he could not get hold of Molson, Ginter felt he no longer needed shares in the Vancouver hockey team, which he had proudly called "my team." Ginter now had a different explanation as to why he wanted the Canucks. He said hockey was Canada's national sport, and it should be controlled by Canadians. However, his 37,000 shares for which he paid $670,000 were far from being "Canadian controlled." The majority shareholder was Medicor, a Milwaukee consortium which held some 600,000 shares. It took some time before Ginter could shed his shares after he decided to abandon plans to own a hockey team. When he did get rid of them, he was dissatisfied and promptly filed a law suit against the club's directors, claiming damages for fraud or negligence as a result of a $3 million stock transfer from Northwest Sports Enterprise Limited — official owner of the Canucks — to Medicor, Northwest's parent company.

Ginter charged Northwest Sports did not fully disclose its financial position at the time it offered shares to the public. The suit was duly filed, but it took a long time to be resolved. When it was, Ginter lost. Mr. Justice Richard Anderson ruled Ginter had not suffered any losses as a result of his investment in the hockey club but had, in fact, made a profit when he sold his shares. Ginter had alleged that when he had bought the shares, he had done so based on information in a "fraudulent prospectus" published by Northwest Sports Enterprise Limited. The court was told Ginter had bought the shares in December of 1970 and sold them to Senator Ed Lawson for $707,000 three years later. Justice Anderson ruled Ginter was not entitled to hold shares to make a capital gain and at the same time hold Northwest Sports liable for interest on the investment. Ginter shrugged off the result and turned his attention back to brewing beer.

14

GINTER'S EXPANSION INTO ONTARIO was accompanied by a great publicity campaign. He praised the Tory government of Bill Davis for its progressive attitude toward industrial expansion and added he would improve the province's industrial might as well as create employment. Then, nothing was heard about the project, and anyone who asked Ginter how things were coming along would be told with a smile that things were going according to plans. The big let-down came when the Davis government decided to play by different rules than Ginter had anticipated. In 1972 Ginter announced he was cancelling plans for expansion into Ontario. Gone was his praise for Premier Davis and his government. Instead, Ginter claimed he was the victim of a "plot" against him. He had, as he said, "about all I can take."

What had happened? The Ontario government decided not to give Ginter a half million dollar grant through the Ontario Development Corporation. Instead it offered a conventional loan at eight per cent interest. Ginter was outraged and insulted. If he wanted a loan he would have gone to the banks and not to the government, he said. He claimed he was being discriminated against, and then he added something new. Ginter wrapped himself

self in the flag and said he was a patriotic Canadian who was going to provide industry to an economically depressed area and felt it was his duty as a Canadian to tell the public "what was happening in Canada and where the taxpayers' money was going."

As a Canadian operating a Canadian company, the province of Ontario should have provided him with a grant, not with a repayable loan. He fretted that he had been unable to see the premier to explain his views and that he could not even get to see any of the premier's advisors. His messages to Davis went unanswered. It was his understanding, Ginter said, that at the time he was refused a grant or forgivable loan, the Ontario Development Corporation was processing some thirty applications for funds from foreign-based companies. "This premier had been urging Canadians to actively participate in the economic life of Canada, but by rejecting my application, he is departing from his own stated policies," Ginter said. When the government said there were already too many breweries in Ontario and the province was saturated with beer, Ginter asked why that, at the time his application was rejected, the government gave Formosa Springs, an American brewer, permission to built a new plant and permission to Henninger of West Germany to brew beer in Ontario.

"In my view the Ontario government is hoodwinking the people of Ontario into believing it is concerned about promoting Canadians in industry and preventing more foreign corporations from acquiring more control of the few Canadian-owned industries that remain . . . if Premier Davis is really interested in promoting Canadian-owned industry, he had a golden opportunity in our case — but he turned us down," Ginter thundered in a statement released to Ontario newspapers.

He could not resist lashing out at the Big Three and handing a bouquet to the Alberta government at the same time. Ginter said the big breweries had told him they would exert extra pressure on the government in Toronto at election time to prevent his brewery being built as they had no intentions of letting Ginter "in on the good thing we have going in Ontario."

"I guess I was pretty naive when I first went into the brewing business. I was told several times and by different people I could not survive in competition with the big guys because they had everything tied up, including governments. I just couldn't believe it possible, but now, after my experience in Ontario, I am beginning to wonder," Ginter stated. Of all the obstacles he encountered in Ontario, Ginter singled out his battles with Brewers' Warehousing Company Limited. This warehousing company was the Ontario government's arm controlling distribution of beer throughout the province, but the big breweries owned it.

A brewing company had to be a member of the company if it wanted to market beer in Ontario. Ginter claimed the government had given the company so much power it had almost total control of retail beer distribution. The provincial government had instructed the company to handle Ginter's beer in Ontario after he had received permission to ship in beer from Manitoba. Permission had been granted in anticipation of Ginter's beer soon being brewed in Ontario. The distributing company added ten per cent to Ginter's product, saying it needed the higher price since the brew was being shipped in from another province. Ginter pointed out the Big Three also shipped in beer from Manitoba but were not subject to this surcharge. The government refused to intervene when this discrepancy was pointed out.

The warehousing company also dictated the standards of construction for the planned Cornwall brewery, insisted on approving architectural plans and even inserted proposed terms for an agreement to prevent sale of Ginter's best-selling Uncle Ben's Malt Liquor. Ginter was willing to pay the extra money because he really was keen on getting into business in Ontario. Aside from beer he also wanted to make wine and soft drinks. Still, he was not willing to take out a loan and, rather than do so, he would cut his losses and pull out altogether.

Ontario, however, was not the only province he pulled out from. While Ben Ginter never had heroes like other people, there was one man he admired greatly: Cecil Rhodes, the British empire builder whose dream it was to colour the map of Africa red, showing it belonged to Great Britain from Capetown to Cairo. Ginter had a similar dream of colouring Canada's beer map red to show Ginter breweries from the Pacific to the Atlantic. And like Rhodes, Ginter thought of setting up scholarships for Canadians of promise, but Ben never took the time to make this part of his dream a reality. As part of his master plan, and unknown to western Canadians, Ginter had planned to move into Newfoundland.

In Newfoundland, the United States military had recently vacated a facility near St. John's which included a large hangar. This building was ideal for conversion to a brewery. Ginter's executives, as well as Ginter, spent considerable time in Newfoundland to arrange a deal with the government of Liberal Premier Joe Smallwood. The Newfoundlanders were quite interested in Ginter's proposal because it would employ people, and Smallwood was eager to sign a contract with Ginter. When everything was ready for signatures, Ginter and his staff went to

Ginter's Uncle Ben Tartan Brewery was the sponsor of racing at
Assiniboia Downs in 1971.

Smallwood's office. The premier handed Ginter a pen, and Ben sat down to affix his name to the document when he was interrupted by Smallwood. The premier looked at Ginter, and said he expected to receive ten cents from every case of beer Ginter sold in Newfoundland. Ginter and his staff were sitting rigidly on their chairs as Ginter asked the premier to repeat what he had just said because he, Ginter, did not seem to have understood. When Smallwood repeated his demand, Ginter got up and told Smallwood that he could not be part to what amounted to a kickback scheme, thanked Smallwood for receiving him, and left. Cash bribery and cash kickbacks were not the coin Ginter dealt in. So ended the plans for a Ginter brewery chain from sea to sea.

Ginter was not a person to linger long in one spot. His brewery in Manitoba needed his attention, and he had been given a licence to build another one in Alberta. When he had gone into Manitoba in 1968, the city of Winnipeg had been so pleased it made Ginter an honorary citizen, and the provincial government had quickly approved all necessary licences. Then the trouble started.

The Metropolitan Corporation of Greater Winnipeg rejected Ginter's application for rezoning in the suburb of St. Andrews, not once but twice. He saw it as another triumph of bureaucracy over free enterprise and he promptly announced that if Winnipeg did not want his brewery, there were plenty of other towns which would welcome him. Before he made the move to change to Brandon, the municipality of Transcona on Winnipeg's outskirts invited him to look around and indicated to Ginter that he would be accommodated as far as possible. Ginter found the ideal place for a brewery, a building well located and ready to be taken over. Researching the land registry, he found the property was the former Catelli Foods Limited plant owned by Ogilvie Flour Mills Company Limited of Montreal. Ogilvie, it turned out, was a subsidiary of Labatt Brewing Company Limited, Ginter's arch enemy and competitor.

Getting hold of the building would call for some special strategy. He knew Labatt would never sell to Uncle Ben's Industries, so Ginter resorted to a simple trick to get what he wanted. Instead of Uncle Ben's Industries or Tartan Brewery making the offer for the empty structure, Ginter used a trucking company he controlled to buy the building. B and Z Transport Limited was named after two long-time and trusted employees, Walter Betcher and Lloyd Zapf. The offer was accepted, and Ginter owned his rival's building for $800,000. A major law suit was filed immediately afterwards.

A Winnipeg real estate company claimed Ginter failed to pay real estate commission on the deal. The case was heard before Mr. Justice John Solomon of the Court of Queen's Bench. Ginter said he had agreed to pay commission when he first made an offer of $500,000. He had been informed a federal department had also set its sight on the property and had offered $750,000. At that point, Ginter told the judge, he had terminated the service of the realtor, and B and Z Transport Limited had bought the building without an intermediary. The realtor claimed Ginter had been dishonest in juggling names of directors and legal entities to hide the real purchaser from the real estate firm and had done so to deceive the plaintiff.

Mr. Justice Solomon disagreed and ruled he was convinced Ginter did all his juggling to hide the fact he was buying the building, not to deceive the realtor but to prevent Labatt finding out who was buying its property. Labatt, the judge was certain, would have never sold to Ginter. Solomon, however, stressed he did not condone such juggling, but "Ginter was not the only one doing it." He noted that as far as the public was concerned, Catelli Foods Limited was the building's owner. "In fact, it was not the owner, because Catelli was controlled by Ogilvie which in turn was owned by Labatt. There was little difference between the juggling of John Labatt Limited and the juggling of Ben Ginter," the judge said, ruling in Ginter's favour. Ginter was highly pleased and saw this as a victory in his battles with the Big Three. He was ready to brew beer in Manitoba.

Ben Ginter turned his attention to Alberta. He lavished praise on the Conservative government, just as he had done on the Davis government in Ontario. This was rather prophetic because this praise would change into denouncements of Premier Peter Lougheed, just as had happened with the Davis government. Whenever events turned against him, Ginter would look for a scapegoat. It happened in Cornwall and would happen in Edmonton and Winnipeg. It was the familiar Ginter pattern which coloured all his business dealings.

At the moment Ginter praised Lougheed for his foresight in establishing new industry and, within thirty days, approving a loan of a half million dollars to him. In October 1971, Ginter turned the first sod in a ground-breaking ceremony at Red Deer, a city halfway between Edmonton and Calgary. Here he would set up a 70,000 square foot plant, estimated to cost about four million dollars and geared to a production of 200,000 barrels of beer per year. When in full operation, the plant would employ about 70 persons.

Again, matters would not go smoothly for Ginter. He encountered labour problems during construction, causing lengthy delays in construction, and then again when everything was ready to start up. The Alberta unions now insisted Ginter stick to an agreement made earlier which called for area workers to be employed at the new plant. As there was a shortage of skilled brewery workers in central Alberta, Ginter had signed an agreement under which he would retrain bricklayers, carpenters, and other suitable workers who had worked on the construction of the Red Deer brewery at his facility in Prince George, British Columbia. According to Ginter it was not a satisfactory arrangement, but a number of workers were trained for about six months in Prince George.

There may have been good reasons for this agreement, but Ginter failed to see them. To him it was a costly undertaking, training workers in another province. When he balked on complying with the agreement, organized labour started to put pressure on to such an extent that Ginter offered to turn over the plant to the provincial government for the price of his investment. As Ginter grew more disenchanted with Peter Lougheed, he hinted that it was the Alberta government which had forced him to train Alberta workers in British Columbia. The accusations were false, but made good impressions on the public and some unions. Lougheed never bothered to correct Ginter's statements.

Meanwhile, soft drinks were the only products made in the Red Deer plant to be sold in Alberta and Saskatchewan. This caused new problems. Ginter's soft drinks were marketed in returnable beer bottles. The Saskatchewan Brewers Association paid twenty cents for a dozen empties of most drink bottles, but would not accept Ginter bottles. Usually, pop bottles could be returned for five cents each and twenty cents for large bottles. Only one bottle depot in North Battlefort would accept Ginter's bottles and even then would pay only one cent per bottle. The situation was highly confusing, and consumers did not like it when they paid a five-cent deposit, but received only one cent back.

Ginter was told by both the Alberta and Saskatchewan governments to use proper pop bottles or stop making soft drinks. Strangely when the Red Deer plant finally produced beer, the pop disagreements seemed to fade.

15

G INTER, HOWEVER, MANAGED TO STUMBLE from crisis to crisis, each costing him money. By the end of the 1960s, he had become disenchanted with living in Prince George, where he knew he was not appreciated. He moved to Vancouver, where he lived in a suite in the Rembrandt Hotel, gained considerable weight, and worked all hours of the day and night. He increased his drinking. He did make several trip to Las Vegas, Nevada to relax playing poker, the pastime he had picked up in his youth.

His plans called for building a new brewery in Richmond, a Vancouver suburb. He had been forced to set up his own beer distribution network in British Columbia when Pacific Brewers Warehouse Company (PBW) had rejected his application to join. PBW explained Ginter had demanded to become a full member, asking for equality in running the operation, although he commanded only six per cent of total beer sales in British Columbia.

When Uncle Ben's distribution system was in place, PBW refused to handle his bottles, or, if they took them at their depots, they would not return the empties to Ginter. As a result, Ginter was running short of bottles just as he started to market the new malt liquor. He scouted everywhere to find a supply. *The Prince*

George Citizen reported in May 1969 that Ginter was looking for about 240,000 dozen empty bottles, and within a week some 5,000 dozen had been turned in at two special depots in Prince George. Ginter paid thirty cents for his own dozen of empties and twenty cents for other brands. Ginter claimed it was not PBW withholding his bottles from him that caused the shortage, but that the new malt liquor beer was so "hot" that he could not keep up with the demand. He pleaded with beer lovers to return empties at once and not to wait until they had accumulated a few dozen. In a show of humour Ginter joked that it was a good thing he had introduced malt liquor and not the Big Three.

"If they had, you would pay a premium just like you did on canned beer," he laughed. Former Lands, Forest and Water Resources Minister Ray Williston credits Ginter with initiating the 'open beer sales' in provincial liquor stores. For years customers had to walk up to a wicket in a liquor store and order their beer, pay for it, and pick it up another window. Most people just asked for beer, not a brand name; liquor store employees would hand them a case of the more popular brand or, as Ginter charged, they would hand out the brand they had been told to favour or which they preferred to drink themselves. The customer had no choice but to accept it because in a liquor store the employee was king, not the customer. Williston said Ginter suggested to him that beer should be stacked on the floor and customers could pick their own, choosing the brand they preferred by simply looking at the cases. Williston thought it was a good idea and he passed it on to Attorney-General Robert Bonner whose ministry was in charge of liquor matters. Bonner thought it was a good idea, too, and he ordered that stores initiate the new method. It helped boost the sale of Ginter's beer and is still used in liquor stores today.

By this time Ginter had purchased a winery in the Okanagan and pricing of his products was very much on his mind. This time he was fighting with the Growers' Marketing Board which he claimed was dictating the price vintners paid for grapes. He said his company, Mission Hill Wines Limited, had offered growers $170 per ton of grapes, but the marketing board demanded $174 per ton and refused to allow Ginter's representative to present the company's proposals to the growers. "They are absolutely dictatorial about this," Ginter said. He got in touch with provincial agricultural minister Cyril Shelford and also met the press to air his grievances.

"The way marketing boards, at least this one, operate is not justified, and I offered an alternative but was turned down," Ginter complained. What he wanted to do was to hold face to face meetings to negotiate a price; and, if no agreement could be reached, he wanted a government mediator, but the board was not listening. When grapes were ripe, the growers' board demanded $212 per ton and the wine makers offered $130.

Ginter said he was sorry for the growers because they did not have the financial backing to hold out for long, and he suggested government should help them to acquire more acreage to grow grapes. He outlined his thoughts about this matter:

"A family man must take home at least $10,000 a year to live on and that would require a minimum of fifty acres, but they are given five acres." He lambasted the government for a regulation that called for 65 per cent of all ingredients used in the wine to be

Ben, on the left, is surrounded by businessmen at a lunch with an international flavour in Vancouver.

produced in the province to qualify for sale in British Columbia as a native wine. "That leaves a winery no choice as to where to buy grapes and lets the marketing boards set artificially high prices," Ginter said. Again, officials took no notice of his complaints.

At this time Ginter was involved in so many enterprises that it took more cash than he had to operate. He did not want to go to the banks for loans, so instead he turned to the public. He announced he wanted to sell 49 per cent of his holdings in the beer and wine industry which he estimated to be worth between $17 million and $18 million. He would retain a 51 per cent equity, leaving him unencumbered to make decisions without having to ask anybody else's permission. "This protects me in case any of the other breweries wants to take me over," he pointed out. Here again, he compared himself with the Molson family, whose empire could not be taken over as long as the family held the share majority. In Ginter's case it was not a family business, but an empire that centred totally on the persona of Ben Ginter.

He was enlarging his brewery in Prince George to a capacity double the 200,000 barrels annually he was presently brewing. His Richmond plant was to produce between 300,000 and 450,000 barrels a year. He would employ about 150 persons in the new brewery. He knew that, by locating in Richmond, he would be much closer to the American Pacific Northwest which he considered a ready-made market for his products.

In July 1971 Ginter got lucky again. Some 250 brewery workers at Labatt and Molson in Vancouver and New Westminster walked off their jobs. Ginter immediately ordered an increase in beer production, only to run right into new government regulations restraining him. The government had ordered the four still-producing breweries, three others as well as Ginter's, not to try to fill the gap left by the strike. The result was a sixty-five per cent reduction in beer production in the province. Hotel operators had also been told not to make larger beer orders than they did in pre-strike days. The liquor board's explanation was that it had anticipated a shortage, but wanted to assure the public that there was a good supply for the over-counter sales. These sales, of course, were handled mostly by government liquor stores and not hotels.

"This is unbelievably asinine," Ginter said. He called on the public and the hotel operators to ignore the board's edicts because they might be dry in a short time while breweries were sitting on their beer, unable to sell it. "We are told we cannot sell more beer, even though some of us are running at half the brewing capacity. I hope beer lovers, brewers, and the hotels won't stand for this stupidity," he told the press. He also complained he was not allowed to ship in beer from Manitoba. The beer drinking public was not amused, and the resulting clamour forced the liquor control board to change its mind. Ginter got grudging permission to bring beer from the Transcona brewery and even to import American beer, should it become necessary. Ginter at once arranged to have some 60,000 cases shipped from Manitoba, and he told the board he could ship 20,000 cases daily for as long as it was needed.

While Ginter profited handsomely from the strike, he still needed more money to finance the building of his Richmond plant. He now offered to the public 30 per cent of his shares in Uncle Ben's Industries, leaving him in a majority position since he personally owned 95 per cent of the stock. The other five per cent were listed on the stock exchange and were valued at $8 a share, not that they were often traded. Included in his offer were parts of Ginter's holdings in the Okanagan winery, the Prince George brewery, and the site of the future Richmond brewery which Ginter now said would be able to produce about 600,000 barrels per year. These assets were valued at about $7 million. Ginter was also willing to re-package the whole deal to include the breweries in Alberta and Manitoba, bringing the value to about $14 million.

In the meantime, Ginter kept crusading against government

control over beer prices and most other government regulations regarding beer. In 1972 the British Columbia voters turfed out the Socred government under W.A.C Bennett and elected the New Democrats led by Dave Barrett. Ginter was not sorry to see the Socreds go. They had been good for him in the beginning, just as he had been good for them. But as far as Ginter's interests in the brewing industry were concerned, they had been more of a hindrance than a help. He hoped for better things from the "Socialist Hordes."

The New Democrats had barely become used to sitting on the government side of the House when Ginter sprung into action. One of his first acts was to see Premier Barrett to collect a debt. Ginter had submitted a bill of nearly $5 million to the provincial government for work done for the provincially-owned Pacific Great Eastern Railway, now known as BC Rail. The bill went unpaid for nearly five years. Dave Barrett was not only the premier, but also the finance minister and board chairman for the railway. Ginter was accompanied by Joe Rinaldi when he entered Barrett's office in Victoria.

Dave Barrett was an informal man, and he had his shoes off with his jacket hanging on his chair. The two men greeted each other cordially. Ginter stated his business. Barrett said he was fully aware of the outstanding debt and offered to pay Ginter $600,000 within one week if Ginter dropped all further claims to more. Ginter was upset, but Barrett pointed out that they both knew the bill was inflated and that this would come out if public action were taken. Ginter finally agreed, but could not let it go without one more try. When he walked out he turned at the door and said,

"Mr. Premier, at least pay me interest on this money. After all, the bill has been outstanding for five years." Barrett stuck to his offer of $600,000.

Ginter announced he had "definite assurance" from the new Attorney General Alex MacDonald that a recommendation would be made to the liquor control board to allow breweries to set their own prices. Ginter was excited over this idea because it had always been one of his aims to free the industry from government control as far as pricing was concerned. "I am sure there was no misunderstanding," Ginter said when he visited Prince George, "he [the attorney general] did not make any commitment that the board would act on the recommendation, but he agreed breweries should have the right to set their own prices just like wine makers. Where is the difference between wine and beer? Is beer a worse evil?" MacDonald did not take long to put a damper on Ginter's enthusiasms. He said he could not recall the specific topic discussed with Ginter or even when he had met with him. The attorney general said it seemed Ginter had made some representation but no commitments were made on his part.

"If he has made statements that he received any commitments from me, he is talking a blue streak," MacDonald said when he heard of Ginter's statements in Prince George. But Ginter was not to be deterred.

"My lawyer and I sat with the attorney general for a long time on January 17 [1973] and he gave me to understand beer prices would be freed as soon as the liquor board could make it official," Ginter said. To him such a move made sense because there was no price control on wines, and he believed the beer price control was a political tool of the Socreds. How else could it be explained, he said, that a beer in Prince George should cost the same as in Vancouver if the beer were made right there in Prince George.

"That's forcing the Prince George beer drinker to subsidize the Vancouver beer drinker," he mused. But he did not add that it would be Vancouver doing the subsidizing if the beer were shipped to Prince George from Vancouver. As far as Ginter was concerned Vancouver beer was not needed in Prince George. He would look after the thirst up in the North. . . . He also pointed to Alberta and Manitoba where he was allowed to set his own prices. Ginter was sure he could reduce beer prices by about twenty cents per dozen and sell a twenty-five gallon keg about three dollars cheaper than the going price of $41.30 per keg.

Ginter, however, appreciated one innovation the New Democrats made: the establishment of neighbourhood pubs. This broke the monopoly of the hotels in selling beer and added more outlets where he could sell his product. The province's first neighbourhood pub was opened in 1972 in McLeese Lake, the place where Ginter had worked his on first road construction contract after breaking another monopoly.

As glad as he was to see the Socreds defeated, his appreciation of the New Democrats did not last long. He did not like their labour legislation and a number of other laws the NDP brought in. They were far too socialistic for Ginter. By the time the new elections rolled around in 1975, Ginter, again, had threatened to sell all his holdings in the province. However, when Social Credit was returned to power under Bill Bennett, he immediately stated he was reconsidering. He had already sold about $1 million worth

Ben, in an expansive mood, in his study at his Prince George estate.

of equipment in a beginning to shut down his British Columbia operations. After election day, December 11, 1975, he said the people's decision to go for another free enterprise government gave him renewed hope and he would stay in British Columbia. "I was tired of fighting a lost cause when I announced I would be leaving. Everybody gets tired when you fight for a lost cause especially when the fight is for the good of employees, not for my own good," Ginter said. He hoped the new government would bring in new labour legislation, and he called for "cleaning out the labour relations board," along with the purging of some of the current labour leaders in the province.

"All I am saying, the government should see if the labour leaders are qualified for their jobs. Even though I have been hurt financially by the disputes with those labour leaders, it is the rank and file union members who suffer the most from their leaders' stupid decisions. The government should immediately investigate the affairs of some of the unions and completely clean out the labour board. The decisions made by that board should be taken to an unbiased court. Right now it is a kangaroo board packed with union representatives." It was a familiar tune Ginter was singing reminding the public of his initial admiration for new governments and his disenchantment soon after. It happened in Ontario, in Alberta and in Manitoba, and now, in British Columbia. While Ginter was planning to expand his empire in British Columbia, his ventures were not as solid as they appeared to be. Concentrating on the beer business with his characteristic single-mindedness of purpose, he had neglected his other interests. Added to this was a general reduction in major public construction projects throughout the province.

16

GINTER ALWAYS PROUDLY STATED HE WAS financing all his enterprises without major involvement by the banks. But as the cash flow slowed, he did borrow, and he would later say this was his biggest mistake. He considered that borrowing from the banks would leave him wide open to attacks from businesses bigger than himself. Whenever he borrowed he was able to assure lenders that his assets were far larger than his debts. There never was a reason for a lender to worry, he said, but problems were looming. Ginter lost all admiration for the government in Alberta, stating publicly that the sooner the New Democrats would throw out the Conservative government of Peter Lougheed the better off Albertans would be. This outburst was prompted by Lougheed's decision to ban the sale of soft drinks in beer bottles, an old problem Ginter thought had long been laid to rest.

Ben Ginter also faced opposition from the Alberta Federation of Labour which did not like the way he operated and called for a boycott of Ginter products. His investment in his Alberta plant amounted to more than $4 million, of which some $150,000 was tied up in equipment and supplies for making soft drinks. Now he again offered the plant to the government and said he would be happy to get out for cost. He claimed the government had bowed to pressure from organized labour and the other breweries in banning soft drinks in beer bottles. Of course, the government did not take him up on the offer and Ginter kept brewing in Red Deer.

In Manitoba things were not going too well, either. Ginter accused the liquor control authorities there of favouring the "hidden monopoly" of the Big Three. But a spokesman for Manitoba hotels said Ginter was wrong because hotels were required by law to carry all major brands in their beer parlours. Ginter said his Transcona plant was in trouble because the hotels would not sell his beer. The hotels countered that there was hardly a demand for his products, so how could they sell them?

Ginter's constant complaints in the media were widely reported as stories about Ginter always made good copy. However they left a bitter taste among governments and much of the public, and as a result, beer sales were falling not only in Manitoba but also in Alberta and British Columbia. Lower sales resulted in lower cash flow, and Ginter had to muster all his entrepreneurial skills as well as those of his staff to stay afloat.

Ginter, the champion of free enterprise, suddenly called on the government in Victoria to set beer quotas to force hotels to order at least ten per cent of their beer from Uncle Ben's. To those who knew Ginter, it was a strong signal that he was in trouble. The public was plainly rejecting his brew. Ginter threatened again to close the Prince George brewery and shift all his operations to Richmond. He was willing to move key employees from the Interior to the Lower Mainland. Not many were interested in the offer.

Ginter started to really believe the public would be best served by a quota system because it would keep the independent breweries alive. He claimed that "international monopolies" had bought up almost "every brewery in Canada." The truth, however, was that a quota system would not have helped Ginter with his current problems because people would not drink his beer in any appreciable quantities. Hotels had to return unsold beer which then had to be poured down the drain. Ginter's idea that a quota would give the public a greater choice of brands was invalid because nobody wanted to buy his products. People simply did not like "Ginter beer" anymore.

Labour problems never seemed to end for Uncle Ben. Several union members had been promised jobs at the new Richmond brewery when Ginter closed a soft drink operation there because of financial problems. Their union accused Ginter of having reneged on this promise, and one day a number of these former employees occupied the plant. When the employees refused to leave the premises, Ginter called in security guards and had them removed by force. Union officials said Ginter had called on his private goon squad. The workers appealed for help to the British Columbia Federation of Labour and that organization declared all Ginter products "hot," meaning no union member in the province would buy them or even handle them.

This created a curious situation for Ginter's brewery employees in Prince George. The workers were members of the United Brewery Workers Union and therefore members of the Federation. They were producing beer on one hand and boycotting it on the other. A stock of about 200,000 gallons and some 40,000 cases of bottled beer was at hand in the plant, which could not be moved out and therefore could not be sold. Ginter closed down the brewery instead. He was furious with the union and threatened to sue business agent Ed Glasser personally. Ginter felt Glasser was responsible for the "hot" edict, thereby destroying the operation. Glasser immediately threatened a counter-suit if Ginter kept insisting it was Glasser's fault that the Federation was boycotting Uncle Ben's products.

Ginter had written a letter to the union in which he said:

"I feel it is my duty to remind you again that in my opinion you are involved in the restraint of trade and conspiracy determined to cause us to go into bankruptcy. I would remind you that unless we can get our products on the Christmas market the damages we will suffer will be in the millions and we will have to dump several hundreds of thousands of gallons of beer. I beg you to reconsider as I worked hard to build up this organization and the only pleasure I have been able to get in return is to see the operation grow instead of seeing it destroyed for no real reason."

Glasser strongly rejected Ginter's accusation of being responsible for the "hot" edict. He said he went along with the Federation's decision only after failing to dissuade the Federation. "I argued strongly that it should not be put on," he said, "I said that if they want to label Ginter's products 'hot' we would have to support it. As members of the Federation we have to support any edict. We are stuck in the middle and Ginter keeps taking a run at us. He is trying to play one union against the other." He also pointed out that even if the brewery workers' union had not supported the decision, liquor store employees could not have touched any hot Ginter beer. But Ben Ginter was outraged and kept saying the strike was illegal in spite of a ruling by the labour relations board that it was not.

"This illegal strike is a conspiracy between the unions," Ginter said "They are trying to get me to knuckle under or break me, whichever comes first." He felt compelled to sue the union because of the great losses he suffered during the strike. He estimated these losses at at least a quarter of a million dollars. "I'll sue sometime in January or February, and it will be in the millions. In the meantime, I have no income and have had none for the past four months. I think I'll go on welfare."

Events overtook Ginter's schedule with the dawning of January 29, 1976. The three men who appeared at Ginter's Prince George headquarters on that cold January morning were employees of Dunwoody and Company, a well-known Vancouver firm of accountants, and their boss Harold S. Sigurdson had been appointed receiver-manager of Ginter's holdings on behalf of the Canadian Imperial Bank of Commerce (CIBC).

Ginter had been presented with a demand note by the bank only hours after he had been contacted by telephone informing him the bank was calling a note in the amount of $3.9 million. Ginter asked for time to raise the money, but the bank refused and asked the courts for a receivership order. Since Ginter no longer lived in Prince George, he had to be kept informed of the actions there by telephone. At the same time as the takeover took place in Prince George, Ginter's holdings elsewhere were also being placed in receivership. The receivers swooped down on his assets in Richmond, Red Deer, Kelowna and Winnipeg. It was an all-out assault and paralyzed Ginter's operations. Ben was stunned and, predictably, angry.

The three men in Prince George introduced themselves as a Mr. Orton, a Mr. Durant, and a Mr. Barney to Louise McCormick, Ginter's executive assistant. She was informed that both the construction company and the brewery were as of that moment under their management and the men fired all employees. They were re-hired seconds later. There were few people on the premises of the construction company and only three at the brewery, which was not operating because of the continuing labour dispute. Road construction also had declined in the last few years and much of the equipment sat idle. One of the first major acts of the receivers was to nail huge wooden signs to the buildings informing the public of the receivership and warning that nothing must be removed from the premises by anyone. They also changed every lock. Ginter's first reaction was one of incredulity and then one of extreme anger. True to his reputation for taking anyone he felt had wronged him to court, he felt this was a situation which which left him no other choice but to turn to the courts. He threatened immediate court action against CIBC and the receivers. Calling the note at this time was totally unnecessary, Ginter claimed. He charged publicly that it was a conspiracy between the CIBC and the Big Three breweries, Molson, Carling-O'Keefe and Labatt, who wanted him out of the beer business.

"Here is the proof," Ginter thundered the next day, pointing out that the chairman of the board of Labatt's breweries, John Moore, was also a member of the board of directors of the CIBC. Ginter's statements were inflammatory and libelous, but it is curious to note that neither the breweries nor the CIBC ever threatened to counter-sue or asked the court to stop Ginter from making these accusations. Many people believed Ginter's conspiracy theory, because similar cases had happened in other industries, where a seat on the board of a bank had resulted in the killing of a competing business. To Ginter the links between the breweries and the banks were no coincidence, although everyone else involved denied the allegations. The CIBC maintained that its position at Uncle Ben's Industries was at risk. A bank spokesman said Ginter's company was not viable. A few years after Ben's death, the CIBC submitted an affidavit to the British Columbia Supreme Court stating that Ginter's three main companies had been in arrears with interest payments in the amount of $83,812 on the day the note was called.

At the time of the takeover by a receiver, however, Ginter at once went on the offensive. "The sum I owe is not $3.9 million, it is only $3.6 million," he told the press. Within days he called on the federal government in Ottawa and the provincial administrations in Edmonton, Winnipeg, and Victoria to guarantee loans so he could pay off the bank. He would raise the money by selling off assets. But he was concerned, even worried, that CIBC would not accept government guarantees. He believed the CIBC was under pressure from the national brewing industry. He need not have worried, as none of the three governments even replied to his call for help.

Ginter was also unhappy with the choice of receiver. He did not like Harold Sigurdson whom he had known since he bought the Prince George Brewery in 1962. At that time the plant had also been in receivership, and Sigurdson had been the appointed receiver. The bank which had placed the operation in receivership, of course, had been the Canadian Imperial Bank of Commerce.

While trying for government help, Ginter was not idle. He checked every other source to raise money but met with refusals everywhere he turned. Financial institutions were adopting a wait-and-see attitude because details surrounding the calling of the loan were not widely known. With the caution banks usually display when even the slightest hint of any possible insolvency becomes public, they refused to lend Ginter money for a bailout.

Ginter questioned the timing of the calling of the note and the subsequent receivership. He had borrowed the money only one year earlier which he needed for his Uncle Ben's Industries Limited. This company was listed at the Vancouver Stock Exchange. Ginter owned about 85 per cent of the equity. It was the first time Ginter had borrowed heavily and the loan amounted to $5.5 million from CIBC. The borrowed money was to be secured by debentures spread over all his holdings. It was to be used to set up his own beer distribution system away from the co-operative set up by the Big Three. Part was also to be used to complete construction of the new brewery at Richmond.

"We have always met our interest payments. I could have sold construction machinery, and if they had given me sixty days, I could have had the money," Ginter said. He firmly believed CIBC had been panicked into calling the loan. Since he was making payment, he speculated, the bank was worried that he would be able to retire his debt and remain in business, thereby remaining a thorn in the sides of the Big Three. Ginter said he was not a threat to the Big Three. He was convinced that they were worried he would set a precedent as he had done in the road construction industry when he destroyed a small cartel which up to then had done all provincial highways construction. He never wavered in his belief that he would get out from under his problems; he had always managed before. But the receivership changed Ginter as a person.

He had always been single-minded in the pursuits of his goals and put all of his considerable drive to succeed into these pursuits. Now he lost interest in all but the defeat of the receivership. He wanted to see Sigurdson humbled and preferably out of business. Ever since he started on his way to success, almost thirty years earlier, Ginter had regarded each of his endeavours as a personal challenge. He saw himself as pioneering new grounds and he threw his considerable energy into each of his enterprises. Now he concentrated on defeating the receiver with the same energy.

Ginter began to regard Sigurdson as his personal nemesis, and he threw every obstacle he could devise into Sigurdson's path. He objected to every action the receiver took with the property. That this was costing him large sums of money was immaterial. Ginter's goal was to get back what he had built with his sweat and Sigurdson stood in his way. Ginter believed Sigurdson took pleasure in ruining him and pointed to the problems his Executive Assistant Louise McCormick encountered. McCormick had been employed by the receiver to work in her former capacity, but was soon fired. The receiver said she had resisted an attempt by the receivers to include some of Ginter's private possessions in the receivership. Sigurdson added it was also a matter of restructuring manpower requirements and McCormick was no longer needed. Ginter said she had been correct in her actions to protect his private possessions. She sued for wrongful dismissal, but discontinued her suit when Ginter died.

At the same time Ben was greatly bothered because his debt increased daily. Although beer was sitting in his warehouse at the brewery in Prince George, he could not sell it because of the B.C. Federation of Labour's "hot" edict against all Ginter products. Construction equipment sat idle because there were few contracts for Ben Ginter Construction Company Limited or, for that matter, any construction company. The Socred boom years of road construction and dam-building were over. "All expenses the receivership incurs are charged to me. It costs me about $5,000 each week. So, the sooner I can pay off the loan, the sooner I can do things my way," he told friends.

Ginter, as well as Sigurdson, started to hunt for buyers for the brewery in Prince George. All kinds of offers were received. Not one proved to be acceptable. Sigurdson succeeded in one area where Ginter had failed; he re-opened the brewery on February 11, 1976 after settling the labour dispute. Sigurdson reached an agreement with the Retail, Wholesale and Department Store Union on behalf of Uncle Ben's Industries after eight months of dispute between Ginter and the union. Now a new contract was signed and the edict lifted. In Prince George the thirty-six employees at the brewery went back to work under the receiver. At this time some 200,000 gallons of unbottled beer and and about 40,000 dozen of bottled beer were sitting in the warehouse and ready to be sold. The beer had been tested and found drinkable.

With the new collective agreement in place, the brewery became the target of renewed offers for purchase. Ginter declared he was ready to sell, but not at fire sale prices. He went to court to prevent one sale which offered $870,000, less than one-third of the original asking price of $3 million. A realtor, acting for the unidentified buyer, said the offer was made only for the buildings and the land but did not include the brewing equipment.

"At this price the receiver wants to make sure the brewery is never going to operate again," Ginter grumbled and again pointed out that shutting down the brewery for good was the aim of the CIBC who was acting, he felt, on behalf of his competitors.

Vancouver Western Brewing Company, headed by business-man David Thompson made an offer to buy the brewery, but this potential sale ran into snags and was delayed until the Prince George Association for the Mentally Handicapped entered the picture. The Association's executive director, future Socred politician and cabinet member of the scandal-riddled government of William Vander Zalm, Bruce Strachan, announced his association wanted to buy the brewery.

His plans were rather hazy but called for persons under the care of the association to work alongside regular workers and perform tasks within their scopes. Amazingly enough, this plan had the backing of the Prince George and District Labour Council, whose president, Ed Bodner, said the brewery was the livelihood of some forty families and should be kept going under any circumstance. At the time the asking price for the total package, including land, buildings, and equipment, was $1.5 million. Ginter and Sigurdson met briefly with Strachan, but in the end, the association could not come up with the money.

Strachan had hoped for federal job programs to pay for the employment of his charges and the purchase price was to have been raised from private sources and the provincial government.

Many people in Prince George called the plan totally unrealistic. The scheme did not work and Ginter's debt continued to climb. A second creditor added to Ginter's woes. First City lowered the boom on Ginter and demanded payment of $1.5 million. First City also appointed Sigurdson its receiver.

17

GINTER ARRANGED FOR AN AUCTION of heavy equipment to be held in Prince George. It raised about $2 million. Another $500,000 was raised at a Kamloops auction. Noel Smith, the man who sold Ginter his first tractor in 1948, came from Missouri where he now lived. He was one of several hundred bidders and told friends he remembered well when Ginter hitchhiked to his equipment lot in Saskatoon to buy his first piece of machinery. Smith said Ginter and he became partners, and Smith helped him build the Pacific Great Eastern Railway track in the Prince George area. Smith bought several pieces of machinery and predicted Ginter was not finished by a long shot just because of the receivership. "Ben still has a lot of friends and he'll come back, that's for sure," Smith said.

But it seemed Ginter could not win. During the shutdown of the Prince George brewery, much of the market for his beer had been lost. The Big Three had introduced strong beer similar to Uncle Ben's Malt Liquor, and when the Ginter beer reappeared on the liquor store shelves, sales were sluggish at best.

Sigurdson decided to close down operations again. More then 100,000 dozen cases of bottled beer were poured down the drain.

The receiver also made repairs to the plant which Ginter deemed unnecessary and a waste of his money, but Sigurdson insisted the repairs had been ordered by the Workers Compensation Board. Ginter charged the repairs, if they had to be done, could have been carried out while the plant operated. By the mid-summer of 1976, the plant was closed, and every employee laid off. Ginter's shortage of cash was more acute than ever.

In 1977 Ginter came up with a novel idea to raise money. He offered shares in his enterprise for bottle caps. For every 200 of his bottles caps, he offered a block of ten shares. He was optimistic that his beer was soon to be on the market again. "This offer will be good until forty per cent of my holdings are bought up by the public," Ginter declared. An individual's investment for the shares would be $74 for the seventeen cases of beer he had to buy to get the caps.

In British Columbia Ginter hoped to sell 91,800 shares through the caps which translated into about 18,360,000 caps or the sale of 1.5 million cases of beer. The ten shares were worth $200, Ginter said. Albertans were offered 50,000 shares and Ginter reserved 71,800 shares for Manitobans. The liquor administration in Victoria took a very close look at the scheme. No one had ever heard of anything like that before. The government, as represented by the liquor board, found there was nothing illegal about it and the scheme went ahead. Ginter joked that his scheme was less outlandish than the fiscal theories of the Socreds. But the public did not play. Liquor stores reported only a slight increase in sales of Uncle Ben's beer where it was still available. Eventually this scheme along with others silently disappeared.

But Ginter now was able to raise money. Through personal

persuasion and by opening his books to potential creditors, he was able to convince the Royal Bank of Canada and a number of private sources to advance him enough cash to buy back some of his holdings. By selling some more of his construction equipment, he was able to operate the companies he now could call his own again. Several people close to him said it seemed some of his creditors appeared to be convinced of Ginter's conspiracy theory and agreed to help him, lest they should face a similar situation somewhere down the road. He bought back his Red Deer brewery and later the winery in Kelowna. He renamed the winery Golden Valley and sold it in June 1982 for $4 million.

Ginter kept on paying off his debts, but they seemed to keep increasing instead of decreasing. One of the reasons was, of course, that every time Ginter took the receiver to court he had to pay not only his attorney and costs but also the costs of the court and the receiver. Ginter kept complaining Sigurdson and his subordinates had no idea how to run a brewery and he was disposing of Ginter's assets at rock bottom prices. Sigurdson countered that Ginter caused his own problems — and everyone else's — by blocking sales of assets. At a court hearing in Vancouver, Sigurdson testified he could have sold all of Ginter's breweries for $9.7 million to a Japanese group who would also have taken over Ginter's debts. Ginter refused to sell at that price. But it bolstered his claim that his holdings outstripped by far his indebtedness and that there had been no real reason for calling the note in the first place.

"This points out what I have said all along: there was no need for a receiver," Ginter claimed. He told the press that it cost him $656,000 to keep the receiver operating for eleven months. This was a jump from $236,000 for operating costs in the first year of receivership. He was extremely angry about this sharp increase. The receiver had now administered Ginter's assets for more than two years, and Ginter increased his efforts to get out from under the receivership. He had borrowed $2.8 million to buy back the Red Deer brewery and another $810,000 to purchase the Kelowna winery.

There was not enough money to redeem his flagship, the Prince George brewery. Some interested parties had inspected the plant, including a man who claimed to represent Arab oil interests. Ginter personally escorted Dr. Moustapha Samy on a trip to Prince George. Samy claimed he represented a group of investors, mainly the government of Kuwait which was interested in all kinds of businesses anywhere in the world. It was somewhat curious that abstemious Arabs would be interested in a brewery, but Ginter did not care as long as he was offered a good price. While touring the brewery Ginter explained with great patience what role all the machinery and fixtures played in beer making and Dr. Samy nodded dutifully. Later they looked at Ginter's lands and then flew back to Vancouver in Ginter's plane. That was the last Ginter saw — or heard — of Dr. Samy.

By mid-summer of 1978 Ginter had to agree to the sale of the Prince George plant. A consortium headed by Vancouver real estate developer Nelson Skalbania offered $1.55 million and both Ginter and the receiver agreed this was about as much as they were likely to ever get. Ginter, however, agreed only reluctantly.

The former brewery employees were offered their jobs back, and most returned after a federal grant had been received to reopen the plant. The opening took place with much pomp and fanfare in the presence of politicians and local dignitaries. Ginter did not attend. His original Tartan Brewery, then Uncle Ben's, was now the Prince George Brewing Company Limited, and the man appointed to run it was Bob Naismith, formerly employed by Ginter as a property manager. Nick Bennett, a Scottish-born brew-master, was hired to make beer. The name would later be changed first to Old Fort Brewing and then to Pacific Western Brewing Company Limited. Ownership would also change several times. It is now owned by a Japanese company, Pacific Pinnacle Investments Ltd.

This sale, more than anything else, embittered Ginter. The Prince George outfit had been the foundation of his brewing empire. He had nurtured it from 1962 when he took the derelict plant over. Here he had achieved several firsts in the industry, setting examples for the rest of Canada. It was from this plant that his fame as a brewer spread. An American author rated Ginter's Old Blue and Uncle Ben's Malt Liquor brands as among the best beers in the world, a rating Ginter had been very proud of. This quality had come from Prince George, and now it was lost to him.

There was not much left of the rest of the Ginter empire. The construction machinery had been auctioned off, and about a year later, the Richmond brewery was sold to an Alberta group for $2.8 million. This sale spurred Ginter into one of his last big protests, as he considered the price far too low. He said he had negotiated a price of $6 million, but the receiver had ignored him. Ginter's Winnipeg brewery had been sold as a warehouse because no one could be found who wanted to brew beer in Manitoba and thus incur the wrath of the Big Three. Ginter himself had bought the brewing equipment. He had no immediate use for it, but was not about to let it fall into the hands of a competitor. Ginter also felt this equipment would be useful, when he was back on his feet and his empire would make a come-back.

Ginter was not yet off the hook. He still owed money. He estimated legal and receivership costs totalled $3 million. CIBC so far had received $4.5 million on its original note of $3.9 million or, as Ginter claimed, a "mere" $3.6 million. First City received $2.4 million from the receiver toward settling a $1.5 million debt. Operating the companies in receivership took about $5 million, and another $2 million went for taxes and settlement of smaller debts. Ginter claimed he had paid out more than $9 million to the receiver and still could not get his properties back. There were legal claims and some outstanding receiver costs, he was told. Most of the legal claims were initiated by Ginter against Dunwoody and Company. Before any final settlement could be made, the receivers demanded Ginter drop all legal claims. Only then would Ginter get a discharge from receivership.

This whole situation, of course, reflected on his credit rating. While he had been able to borrow money to buy back the Red Deer brewery and the winery in Kelowna, he was unable to obtain bonding for construction jobs. Asking for a performance bond is a common practice and assures the builder — in Ginter's case, the provincial highways department — that the contractor is serious and able to complete the project. Bonding companies seemed to have the same doubts about Ginter's finances as the banks had when they refused to lend him money to pay off the note. But he thought he still had an ace up his sleeve; Mid-West Construction Company Limited, one of his firms, was not in receivership. When he was refused a performance bond for a construction project he had bid on, he offered the company to three of his employees, Louise McCormick, Walter Betcher, and Lloyd Zapf. Ginter would turn the shares over to them and they would pay him when they could. The three were required to put up some security; after all, there were several millions of dollars involved. They were willing to mortgage their homes to the hilt and borrow whatever else they could. But it was not enough. Their equities resulting from the mortgages were insufficient for the bonding company to issue the bond. The plan was dropped.

By then it was 1982. In the spring that year Ginter suffered a heart attack while in Las Vegas. On July 17 he had another severe attack and died in a Richmond hospital at the age of 59.

Through sheer hard work and will-power, Ginter had created one of the largest British Columbia-based industrial empires in the history of the province in less than thirty years. He was the president of and major shareholder in Ben Ginter Construction Company Limited, Ben Ginter Construction (1948) Limited, Argus Construction Company Limited, Ben Ray Bridge Company Limited, Ginter Leasing Limited, Houston Mining Limited, James G Construction Company Limited, Mid-West Construction Company Limited, Imperial Airways Limited, and Brigantines Automotive Limited.

In addition Ginter was president of and major shareholder in Uncle Ben's Industries Limited which owned and operated Uncle Ben's Brewery in Prince George and Uncle Ben's Winery Limited at Westbank, British Columbia. Completing his holdings were a brewery at Richmond, British Columbia, still in the construction stage; Uncle Ben's Breweries of Alberta Limited in Red Deer; Uncle Ben's Brewery (Manitoba) Limited in Transcona just outside of Winnipeg; and Uncle Ben's Beverage Limited, a company which produced and distributed non-alcoholic beverages in British Columbia, Alberta, Saskatchewan and Manitoba. Ginter's personal wealth was estimated at between seven and thirty million dollars.

"At one time I employed more than 9,000 people, but the lawyers and receivers got the profits of my work at the end," Ginter had said. He died believing that after more than six years in receivership, he had paid his debts. Some $19 million had been realized from the operation and sale of his assets, and Ginter had been ready to battle it through the courts once again when he died. His health had deteriorated over the last few years, and the continuing fight over the receivership had taken its toll. Shortly before his death, he ruefully said it had seemed to him he had worked for lawyers and receivers most of the time in recent years.

Ginter gave his last interview to *The Vancouver Province*, two days before his death. He complained bitterly about the laws governing receiverships and the courts. He said receivers could do virtually anything with other people's property without being called to account for their actions. He also repeated his belief in a conspiracy that drove him out of business. "How else can one explain that the CIBC loaned several hundreds of thousands of dollars to Sigurdson to manage my business, while they would not deal with me? There are thousands of receiverships each year and never is a bank or the receiver called to task. Under the law they cannot do anything wrong," he told *The Province*.

He also repeated that his assets at the time the bank called the note in 1976 were sufficient to cover his debts and that the sale of some of these assets would only add to his funds. He said all the

The official portrait of Benjamin George Ginter at the height of his achievements in the 1970s.

problems could have been avoided had there been some sense of fair play involved.

Ginter's body was taken to Minitonas, Manitoba to be buried in the family plot. At the memorial service held in Richmond, the Reverend Phil Gaglardi, the former highways minister, eulogized Ginter: "He was known to all of us as Ben. He was the epitome and the amplification of the Canadian dream. He had the ambition and the determination to do it his way. He gave no quarter and asked no quarter. Our great nation and our province was built by men of his type. He carved out what he wanted and did it on his own terms."

Only about fifty people showed up at the service. Among them were former British Columbia Supreme Court Judge Angelo Branca and Ginter's estranged wife Grace, along with their sons. The service was simple and would have pleased Ginter, with the quiet playing and singing of such fundamental hymns as "Abide With Me," "The Old Rugged Cross," and "He Walks With Me."

Postscript

BEN GINTER TRIED TO EXERCISE HIS DOMINANCE over those around him even after his death. He had often said that if he "couldn't take it with him, he wouldn't be going." Since this was not possible, at least he tried to determine where his money was to go after his death and who would get it.

He had changed his will several times in the last years, and the last version directed that his wife, Grace Myrtle Ginter, would receive $1,000 per month for life or until she re-married, out of an estate close to $6 million. One third was left to divide amongst his six sisters — Adina Kotesky, Olea Heiman, Marian Sibbald, Martha McDonald, Esther Pearson, and Hilda Betcher — as well as with brother Fred and the step-nephew Walter Betcher who had come west with Ginter in 1948 and had stayed with him to the end. The bulk of the estate was left to Ginter's sons, James and Shayne.

Grace Ginter who had been married to Ben for 37 years, but not lived with him since 1968, had never publicly criticized her husband, and had stayed in the background. But leaving her with this paltry allowance was much less than she deserved, and she challenged her late husband's will under the Wills Variation Act, calling for a share of at least fifty per cent of the estate. It took three years before the matter was resolved. In the meantime, Grace Ginter as not totally destitute, as she received $100,000 from a life insurance policy Ginter had taken out some years earlier. She had made the payments over the years since Ginter had regretted taking the insurance out and had stopped making premium payments.

James and Shane had agreed to give their mother the $750 a month each received from the estate and also agreed to give their mother half of whatever the courts would give them. Mr. Justice Harry McKay of the British Columbia Supreme Court ruled that the understanding between mother and sons was not binding on the court, and he ordered that a hearing be held. Among the witnesses called was Phil Gaglardi, the former highways minister, who had been closely associated with Ginter during the heady days of road construction in the province. Gaglardi told the court when he had visited the Ginters in Prince George, they had often talked about how they had started out in the construction business and what role Grace Ginter had played. She had been Ginter's bookkeeper, construction camp cook, as well as mother of the two children.

She had also looked after the ranch, Grace Ginter told the court. She looked after the registration and tattooing of the herd of registered Herefords and tended to the Arabian horses the Ginters kept on the 175 acre Green Valley Ranch. Ben Ginter's role in operating the ranch was called "not much," she testified. Grace Ginter's lawyer, Tom Braidwood, told Mr. Justice McKay that his client had been an integral partner in amassing the family fortune while the other heirs had not been. "She was a wife of 37 years standing. The courts have said that 12 years is a full and complete marriage for the purpose of a division of assets under the Family Relations Act," he said.

Noel Smith, the man who had sold the first Cat to Ben Ginter and had become a partner, testified that when the partnership started out they had bought an old army camp for the crews. "It was cold," Smith said, "but Grace would be up every morning and she'd still be there late at night making sandwiches for the men's lunch next day." Testifying on her own behalf, Grace Ginter said she had moved to Vancouver in 1968 when her husband decided to sell the ranch in Prince George. Ginter was spending more and more time away from home, and with the sale of the Golden Valley Ranch, she saw no reason to remain in Prince George.

"What happened to the marriage at that time? Be as frank as you can," Braidwood told her.

"You mean, as far as Ben's running around is concerned? That was common knowledge for a long time. He did not spend much time with us. He had a girl friend; she lived right across the alley from our townhouse on Yew Street in Kerrisdale (a Vancouver district). He would go and see her but did not have time to come over to see his son," Grace Ginter testified, adding that Ginter had not spent Christmas with his family since 1968.

Mr. Justice McKay in deciding the case, said he agreed that the $1,000 a month left to Grace Ginter was inadequate, and he overruled Ben Ginter's will, handing him his final defeat. The judge said that even the representatives of the eight relatives who had been left thirty per cent of the estate agreed Ginter had failed in his duties to his wife. He ruled the relatives were to receive twenty per cent, while Grace Ginter would get one third, and the remainder should be split equally between James and Shane

Ginter. Mr. Justice McKay singled out Walter Betcher in his statement. He said Betcher had proven a loyal and trusted employee, and it was understandable Ben Ginter wanted to reward this loyalty to him in his will.

The judge put actual figures in his ruling: A sum equal to 3.3 per cent was to go to each of the relatives and Walter Betcher; 33.3 per cent was to go to Grace Myrtle Ginter, while the two sons received the remainder to be paid to them in instalments of five per cent at the age of 21, twenty per cent at age 27 and the balance at age 32.

"By all accounts she was a good wife. It is true they had drifted apart in the later years, but it was a thirty-seven year marriage," the judge said of Grace Ginter. The couple had not lived together for 14 years, but a petition for divorce and a petition for divisions of assets had not been heard at the time of Ginter's death.

With this decision by the British Columbia Supreme Court, Ben Ginter had lost his final battle. The Ginter estate was dissolved and his empire, the efforts of three decades of hard work and relentless drive, faded into the history of the province.

Index

Acapulco (Mexico) 11
Agriculture see BC Ministry of Agriculture
Airplanes, owned by Ginter 44-46, 95-96, 98-99, 111, 179
Airport, in Prince George 33, 36, 44-45
Alaska 33, 62-63, 131
Alaska Highway 33
Alberta 14, 33, 85, 131, 141, 145, 148, 150-152, 158, 161, 163-165, 177,180, 182-183; Calgary 80, 150; Edmonton 27, 57, 80, 150, 170; Lethbridge 8; Red Deer 5-6, 57, 78-80, 150, 165, 168, 178-179,181-182
Alberta Federation of Labour 164
Alcan (company) 21
Alexandra Forest Industries Ltd. 68
Aluminium Company of Canada 21
Americans see United States
Anderson, David 65-66
Anderson, Richard (Judge) 142
Arab investors 179
Arabian horses see Horses
Argus Construction Company 182
Arizona 60
Armstrong, Lew 51-53, 57
Army 4, 7; army camp in Prince George 16, 188
Arrow Dam 22
Assiniboia Downs (horse racing) 147
Attorney-General see BC Attorney-General
Austria 40, 117
B & Z Transport Ltd. 149
Baldy Hughes (radar base) 21
Banks 164, 183; see also Canadian Imperial Bank; Royal Bank
Baptists 1-2, 58
Barney, Mr. 169
Barrett, Dave (Premier) 159-160
BC Attorney-General 31, 115, 127, 130, 139, 154, 160
BC Federation of Labour 166-167, 173
BC Lieutenant Governor 81
BC Ministry of Agriculture 155
BC Ministry of Highways 22, 25, 51, 66;

see also Gaglardi
BC Ministry of Lands, Forests, Water Resources 24-26, 63, 68-70,114-115, 137-139, 154 BC Ministry of Public Works 22 . BC RAIL 18, 159
BC TV 40
Beer see Breweries; Brewing
Ben Ginter Construction Co. 21, 27, 32-34, 71, 73, 173, 182
Ben Ray Bridge Co. 182
Bennett, Bill (Premier)161
Bennett Dam 22, 32
Bennett, Nick 180
Bennett, Richard B. (Prime Minister) 7
Bennett, William Andrew Cecil (Premier) 22, 32, 66, 89, 159
Betcher, Hilda 15, 186
Betcher, Walter 15-16, 149, 182, 186, 189
"Big Three" (national breweries) XIII, 120, 124-125, 128-129, 137-139, 145, 150, 154, 165, 169, 171, 176, 180; see also Carling O'Keefe;Labatt; Molson
Binder, Henry (Hank) 6-7, 60, 140-141
Bodner, Ed 174
Bonner, Robert 31, 115, 139, 154-155
Boyle, Harry 26-27
Braidwood, Tom 187
Branca, Angelo (Judge) 185
Brandon (Man.) 148
Breweries by location, Alberta 5-6, 79, 131, 145, 150-152, 158, 161, 164-165, 177, 179, 181-183; Manitoba 131, 141, 145, 148-150, 158, 161, 165, 168, 177, 180, 182-183; Newfoundland (proposed) 146, 148; Ontario (proposed) 141, 143-146; Prince George B.C. xi, 46-48, 56, 58-59, 78, 86-88, 110, 113-141, 153-154, 157-158, 160- 161, 165-176, 179-180, 182; Richmond B.C. 88-89, 93, 153, 157- 158, 165-166, 180, 182; Saskatchewan 141, 151-152, 183
Brewers' Warehousing Co. 145-146
Brewing industry, beer cans 128-129; bottle caps sold for shares 177; bottle drive 153-154; displays in liquor stores 154-155; equipment 14, 114-

117; neighbourhood pubs 161; public sale of shares 86-88,156-157, 177; quota system 165-166; Royal Commission 80, 138-141; turkey certificates 140-141; see also "Big Three";
Breweries by location; Unions
Bridges, Ben Ray
Bridge Co. 182; Quesnel 33
Brigantines Automotive Ltd. 182
British 146
Burns Lake 49
Burrage Creek 33
Byelorussia 1
Calgary (Alta.) 80, 150
California 104, 133-134
Canada Hotel (Prince George) 120-121, 124, 135-136
Canadian Imperial Bank of Commerce (CIBC) 113, 168-171, 174, 181, 183
Canadian National Railways 76
Canadiens see Montreal Canadiens
Canucks see Vancouver Canucks
Cariboo Brewing Co. 113, 118
Cariboo region 25
Carling O'Keefe; Carling Breweries 52, 120, 128-129, 169
Carling, Stan 82-85
Cassiar 33, 36, 90
Catelli Foods Ltd. 149-150
Catholics 1, 8
Cattermole, Richard 68
Cattermole Timber Ltd. 67-69
Cattle, see Fairs & exhibitions; Green Valley Ranch
Central Fort George 18
Chamber of Commerce (Prince George) 41, 79-80
Chicago (Ill.) 114
CIBC see Canadian Imperial Bank of Commerce
Citizen see Prince George Citizen
CJCI Radio 101
Coates, John 82
Colorado 21
Columbia River 22
Columbus Hotel (Prince George) 16
Conservatives (Progressive Conservative Party, Tories) federal 7, 95-96;in Alberta 150, 164; in B.C. 22; in Ontario 143-144, 150
Construction, 7-8, 14-15, 21, 31, 42, 66,

79, 89-90, 113-114, 163, 169,171-173, 176, 178, 180-182; airport 33, 36; bridges 33, 182; highways 21, 23-26, 32-34, 36, 90; labour disputes 27-28, 151; pulp mills 32, 70-71, 73; project in Alaska 62-63; radar base 21; railway contracts 18, 159-160
Cornwall (Ont.) 141, 146, 150
Court actions see Law suits & court actions
Couvelier, Mel 65
Crown Zellerbach (company) 70
Cuba 10
Curling Club (Prince George) 41
Cutt, Bill 124, 135
Czechoslovakia 131
Daily News see Kamloops Daily News
Dams 21-22, 32, 173
Davis, Bill (Premier) 143-144, 150
Deeks, Harley 128
Depression ("Dirty Thirties") xi, 6-7, 15
Dezell, Garvin (Mayor) 114-115
Drinks see Breweries; Brewing; Soft drinks; Wine
Dunwoody & Company 168, 181
Durant, Mr. 169
Edmonton (Alta.) 27, 57, 80, 150, 170
Edmonton Journal (newspaper) 57
Education, Ginter's 2-3, 6, 146; Ginter's sons 99; school land dispute 101; training of workers 96
Enso-Gutzeit Osakeythio (company) 70
Environment see Pollution
Eurocan Pulp & Paper Co. 70, 72, 79; see also Pulp mills
Europe & Europeans 2, 26, 33, 82, 89, 125, 141; see also Austria; Czechoslovakia; Finnish; Germany; Irish; Italians; Poland; Russia; Scottish; Swedes; Ukraine
Exhibitions see Fairs & exhibitions
Fairs & exhibitions, Calgary 80; Edmonton 80; Prince George 41, 61, 78, 80-82; U.S. 80
Family Relations Act 188
FBI (Federal Bureau of Investigation) 62-63
Finlay Forest Reserve 67-70
Finnish investors 69-70
First City (creditor) 175, 181
Fishing 46-47, 98-99
Florida 8, 10

Forestry, in Ont 6; in Prince George 17-18, 40; timber rights XIII, 67-70; see also Pulp mills
Formosa Springs (U.S. brewery) 144
Forrest, Bill 26
Fort George 18, 24, 63, 139
Fort William (Ont.) 6-7
Fraser River 16
Fuddle Duck (brand name) see Wine
Gaglardi, Jenny 25, 30, 32
Gaglardi, Phillip Arthur XII, 22-25, 30, 32, 51, 58, 66, 111, 185, 187
Gambling 6-7, 85; in Las Vegas 10-11, 99, 153, 182; in Reno 99
German, Howard 75
Germany & Germans 1, 7, 26, 29, 33, 44, 100, 144
Ginter, Ben (Benjamin George) birth & citizenship 1-2; death & will 44, 185-189; dealings with other businesses 36-37, 41-45, 75; education 2-3, 6, 146; employee relations 5-6, 19-21, 41-42, 46, 48, 50-57, 59-60, 91-92, 99-100, 111, 140-141; family relations 3-4, 6-9, 15, 98-99, 186-189; generosity 43-44, 51, 78, 90; home/ranch 39, 62-64, 78, 86, 93, 104-112, 162, 187-188; work habits 4-5, 7, 18-21, 74-75, 87-88, 94, 96; see also Breweries; Construction; Media; Politics; Unions; other subjects throughout
Ginter Construction see Ben Ginter Construction
Ginter, Fred (brother) 1, 3-4, 186
Ginter, Grace Myrtle (nee Peraux, wife) 7-12, 15-16, 25, 30, 32, 82, 97-99, 111, 185-189
Ginter, Henrietta (mother) 1-2, 6, 14-15
Ginter, James (son) 47, 97-99, 108, 185-189
Ginter Leasing Ltd. 182
Ginter, Shane (son) 97-99, 108, 185-189
Ginter, Toefil (father) 1-2
Glasser, Ed 167
Golden Valley Winery 178
Golf & Curling Club (Prince George) 41
Government see Political parties; Politics & government
Grace Finance (company) 69
Grand Trunk Pacific Railway 18, 41
Green Valley Ranch 105, 112, 187-188; see also Ginter, Ben-home/ranch

Growers' Marketing Board 155-156
Hamburger Abendblatt (newspaper) 26
Harkins, Bob 100-101
Hawaii 12-13
Heiman, Olea 186
Henninger (German brewery) 144
Highways 21-26, 30, 32-34, 36, 51, 66, 90, 111, 187; see also Construction
Hockey see Montreal Canadiens; Vancouver Canucks
Hope (B.C.) XII Horses, brother's 4; prize winning Arabians 78, 80, 82-83, 85, 105, 187; racing at Assiniboia Downs 147
Hotels, in Prince George see Canada Hotel; Columbus; Inn of the North; McDonald; Simon Fraser; in Vancouver see Rembrandt
Houston 48-49, 73, 182
Houston Mining Ltd. 73, 182
Hubbard, Jim 5-6
Hudson's Bay (store) 55
Hudson's Hope 32
Hunting 19, 85, 99
Illinois (Chicago) 114
Imperial Airways Ltd. 45, 182
Industrial Progress (magazine) 51
Inn of the North Hotel (Prince George) 101, 110
International Brotherhood of Teamsters 70
International Union of Operating Engineers 27-28, 70-73
Irish 8
Italians 22
James G Construction Co. 182
Japanese 105, 178, 180
Jeffrey, Chester 101-102
Joergensen, Derek 27-28
John Labatt Ltd. see Labatt
Kamloops 22-26, 30, 51, 53, 176
Kamloops Daily News (newspaper) 51, 53
Kamloops Sentinel (newspaper) 26
Kelfor (company) 73
Kelowna 168, 178-179, 181
Kemano Project (Kitimat) 21
Kenny Dam 21
King, William Lyon Mackenzie (Prime Minister) 7
Kitimat XI, 21, 69-72, 79
Kiwanis Club 41

Kotesky, Adina 186
Kuwait investor 179
Kymin Osakeythio-Kynmene Aktiebolag (company) 70
Labatt Brewing Co. (Labatt's, John Labatt Ltd.) 113, 120, 149-150, 157, 169; see also "Big Three"
Labour see Unions
Labourers Union 71
Lands, Forests, Water Resources see BC Ministry of Lands, Forests, Water Resources
Las Vegas (Nevada) 10-11, 99, 153, 182
Law suits & court actions 45, 65, 75-77, 183; brewery sale 173-174, 178, 181; Manitoba land deal 148-150; PILcantrademark 129-131; railway 76; turkey certificates 140-141; unions 75; Vancouver Canucks 142
Lawson, Ed (Senator) 142
Legal actions see Law suits & court actions
Legion, in Prince George 118, 124; in Red Deer 6
Lethbridge (Alta.) 8
Liberals (Liberal Party) federal 7; in B.C. 22, 65-66; in Nfld 146
Lieutenant Governor see BC Lieutenant Governor
Liquor Control Board 47, 120, 124, 126, 129-130, 135-137, 139, 157-158, 160, 177; see also Breweries; Brewing; Wine
Lougheed, Peter (Premier) 150-151, 164
"Mac" see McDonald Hotel MacDonald, Alex 160
MacMillan Bloedel (company) 70
Mafia 137
Manitoba 1-2, 4, 6, 131, 141, 145, 148, 150, 158, 161, 163, 165, 177, 182-183, 185; Brandon 148; Minitonas 2, 4, 6, 8, 41, 60, 185; Rolling River 2; St. Andrews 148; Swan River 1-2, 80; Transcona 148, 158, 165, 182; Winnipeg 6, 17, 59, 76, 80, 95, 141, 148-150, 168, 170, 180, 183
Marketing Board see Growers' Marketing Board
Marwell Construction 72
Masonic Lodge (Prince George) 41
McBride 32
McCormick, Louise 29, 169, 172-173, 182

McDonald Hotel ("Mac," Prince George) 27, 121, 124
McDonald, Martha 186
McKay, Harry (Judge) 187-189
McLeese Lake 24-25, 161
Media, attitude to Prince George 38-40; general dealings with Ginter 27-29, 50-57, 110; see also Newspapers, Radio, Television
Medicore (company) 142 Meistersingers (choir) 40
Mexico 8, 11-12, 98
Mica Dam 22 Mid-West Construction Co. 181-182
Military see Army; Baldy Hughes; Norad; War Milwaukee (Wisc.) 142
Mining, Wenner-Gren project 32
Minitonas (Man.) 2, 4, 6, 8, 41, 60, 185
Mission Hill Wines Ltd. 155; see also Wine Missouri 14, 176
Moffat, Harold (Mayor) 80, 86, 101-102
Molson (company) 59, 120, 128, 141, 157, 169; see also "Big Three" Montreal Canadiens 141
Montreal (Que.) 141, 149
Moore, John 169 Moose, hunting 18
Myllykosken Paperitehas Oy (company) 70
Naismith, Bob 101, 180
National Hockey League 141
Nechako River 16, 21, 113, 125
Nevada, Las Vegas 10-11, 99, 153, 182; Reno 99
New Democratic Party, in Alberta 164; in B.C. 159-161
New Westminster 157
Newfoundland (St. John's) 146, 148
Newspapers see Edmonton Journal; Hamburger Abendblatt; Kamloops Daily News; Kamloops Sentinel; Prince George Citizen; Prince George North?Star; Prince George Progress; Vancouver Province; Vancouver Sun; Vancouver Times; Whitehorse Star
Norad (Colorado) 21
North Battleford (Sask.) 152
North Star see Prince George North Star
Northern Hardware & Furniture Co. 101
Northwest Sports Enterprise Ltd. 142
Northwest Territories 51, 131

Northwood Pulp & Timber Ltd. 73
Ogilvie Flour Mills Co. 149-150
Okanagan 155, 158; see also Kamloops; Kelowna; Westbank; Wine
Old Brew (brand name) see Breweries; Brewing
Old Fort Brewing 180
Ontario 6-7, 141, 143-146, 150, 163; Cornwall 141, 146, 150; Fort William 6-7; Ottawa 76, 170; Toronto 145
Ontario Development Corporation 143-144
Oregon (Salem) 84
Orton, Mr. 169
Ottawa (Ont.) 76, 170
Oy Tampella AB (company) 70
Pacific Brewers Warehouse (PBW) 139, 153-154
Pacific Great Eastern Railway 18, 27, 159, 176
Pacific National Exhibition 80
Pacific Pinnacle Investments Ltd. 180
Pacific Western Brewing Co. XI, 180
Paper see Pulp mills
PBW see Pacific Brewers Warehouse
Peace River, dam 22; forestry license 67
Pearkes, George R. (General) 81
Pearson, Esther 186
Pentecostals 22
Peraux see Ginter, Grace Myrtle
Phoenix (Ariz.) 60
Pilsen (Czechoslovakia) 131
Pine Pass 20
Planes see Airplanes
Poker see Gambling
Poland 1
Police (RCMP) 121-123
Political parties see Conservatives; Liberals; New Democratic Party; Republican Party of Canada; Social Credit
Politics & government 23-25, 29-30, 65-66 (Ginter runs in elections), 67-70, 76, 86, 90-91, 94-96, 120, 124, 126-127, 129-131, 135-140, 157-163, 165-166, 177; see also provinces, political parties & politicians by name
Pollution 96-97
Prince George XI, XII, 5, 13, 15-153, 157-158, 161, 165-168, 170, 173-174, 179; attitude of residents to Ginter 40-41, 63-65, 78-80, 86-94; Cranbrook Hill 104-106; Foothills Boulevard 102,

112; Ginter house 39, 62-64, 78, 86, 93, 104-112, 162, 187-188; Ginter land dispute 101-102; Ginter runs for Council 66; see also Breweries; Dezell (Mayor); Hotels; Moffat (Mayor)
Prince George Airport see Airport
Prince George & District Labour Council 174
Prince George Association for Mentally Handicapped 174
Prince George Brewing Co. 180
Prince George Citizen (newspaper) 26, 28, 50-51, 53, 56-57, 110, 122, 133, 153-154
Prince George Exhibition see Fairs & exhibitions
Prince George North Star (newspaper) 53-57
Prince George Progress (newspaper) 50-53
Prince Rupert 32
Progress see Prince George Progress
Progressive Conservative Party see Conservatives
Province see Vancouver Province
Public Works see BC Ministry of Public Works
Pulp mills XIII, 32, 40, 61, 67, 69-70, 72-74, 79, 122, 137
Quebec (Montreal) 141, 149
Quesnel 33
Radio 80, 100-101
Railways XI, 6-7, 105, 107; BC Rail, formerly Pacific Great Eastern 18, 159; Canadian National Railways 76; Cassiar rail project 90; Grand?Trunk Pacific Railway 18, 41; Pacific Great Eastern Railway 18, 27, 159, 176
RCMP see Police
Recreation see Sports
Recycling see Pollution
Red Deer (Alta.) 5-6, 57, 78-80, 150, 165, 168, 178-179, 181-182
Regina (Sask.) 117
Rembrandt Hotel (Vancouver) 153
Reno (Nevada) 99
Republican Party of Canada 65
Retail, Wholesale & Department Store Union 173
Rhodes, Cecil 146
Richmond 88, 153, 157-158, 165-166, 168, 171, 180, 182, 185

Rinaldi, Joe 59, 62, 133-134, 159
Roads see Construction; Highways
Rolling River (Man.) 2
Roosevelt, Franklin Delano 7
Rose, Rollie 54
Rosenlehner, Hans 44
Rothenburger, Mel 51-53, 57
Royal Bank of Canada 178
Royal Canadian Legion see Legion
Royal Canadian Mounted Police see
    Police
Royal Commission on liquor industry
    80, 138-141
Russia 1, 21
Salem (Oregon) 84
Samy, Dr. Moustapha 179
San Francisco (Calif.) 133
Saskatchewan 19, 141, 151-152, 183;
    North Battlefort 152; Regina 117;
    Saskatoon 14, 176
Saskatchewan Brewers Association 151
Saskatoon (Sask.) 14, 176
Schools see Education
Scottish 180
Shelford, Cyril 155
Sibbald, Marian 186
Sigurdson, Harold 113, 168, 170, 172-
    178, 183
Simon Fraser Hotel (Prince George) 16
Skalbania, Nelson 179
Smallwood, Joe (Premier) 146, 148
Smelter, in Kitimat 21
Smith, George 26
Smith, Noel 14-15, 18, 176, 188
Social Credit Party (Socreds) 22, 24, 65-
    66, 86, 96, 159, 161, 173-174, 177
Soft drinks production, in Alberta 151-
    152, 164-165; in B.C. 166; in Ont. 146
Solomon, John (Judge) 149-150
South Fort George 18
Sports, sponsoring teams 43, 90; see also
    Fishing; Gambling; Golf & Curling
    Club; Hockey; Hunting
St. Andrews (Man.) 148
St. John's (Nfld.) 146
St. Michael's Catholic Hospital
    (Lethbridge) 8
Stanfield, Robert 95-96
Stedman's (store) 55
Stewart-Cassiar Highway 33, 36
Stewart, George O. (Judge) 121-122
Strachan, Bruce 174

Strikes see Unions
Strom, A.W. 51
Strom, Laura 51
Strom, Robert E. 50, 53
Sun see Vancouver Sun
Swan River (Man.) 1-2, 80
Swedes 8, 32
Tabor Mountain 104
Tartan Industries Ltd. see Breweries;
    Brewing
Teamsters see International Brother-
    hood of Teamsters
Television, coverage of Prince George
    40, 80
Terrace 70
Thompson, Aaron 38-39
Thompson, David 174
Timber see Forestry
Toronto (Ont.) 145
Tories see Conservatives
Transcona (Man.) 148, 158, 165, 182
Turner, Cliff 111
Ukraine (Soviet Union) 1
Uncle Ben's Beverage Ltd. see Brewer-
    ies; Brewing
Uncle Ben's Breweries of Alberta Ltd.
    see Breweries; Brewing
Uncle Ben's Brewery (Manitoba) Ltd.
    see Breweries; Brewing
Uncle Ben's Industries Ltd. see Brewer-
    ies; Brewing
Uncle Ben's Malt Liquor (brand name)
    see Breweries; Brewing
Uncle Ben's Winery Ltd. see Wine
Unemployment see Depression
Unions 27-28, 46, 61-62, 65, 70-75, 88,
    93, 96, 135-137, 151, 157, 161-168,
    173-174; Strikes & labour disputes:
    Eurocan 70-72; Houston 72-73; pro-
    vincial beer strike 135-157; Red Deer
    brewery 151; Lower Mainland brew-
    eries 157; union boycott of Ginter
    products 166-168; Prince George dis-
    pute 173
United Brewery Workers Union 166
United States (Americans) awards for
    livestock 80; beer & breweries 14, 118-
    119, 125, 133-134, 140, 144, 157-158,
    180; depression 7; FBI 62; investors 69;
    plane purchased from 46; vacant mili-
    tary site in Nfld 146; see also Alaska,
    Arizona, California, Colorado, Flor-

ida, Hawaii, Illinois, Missouri, Nevada, Oregon, Washington D.C., Wisconsin
University of British Columbia 59, 77
University of Northern British Columbia 40, 112
Vancouver 26-27, 38-39, 44, 63, 67, 72, 85, 88-89, 93, 97-99, 115, 134, 141-142, 153, 156-157, 161, 168, 171, 174, 178-179, 183, 188
Vancouver Canucks 141-142
Vancouver Club 63
Vancouver Island 54
Vancouver Province (newspaper) 26, 38, 183
Vancouver Stock Exchange 171
Vancouver Sun (newspaper) 26, 38-39
Vancouver Times (newspaper) 26
Vancouver Western Brewing Co. 174
Vander Leelie, Peter 52-53, 56-57
Vander Zalm, William (Bill) 65-66, 174
Victoria 22-23, 68, 120, 130, 159, 165, 170, 177
Vienna Schnitzelhaus (restaurant) 44
Vilas Industries Ltd. 141
War 1, 3-4, 7, 15, 21, 32, 94
Washington (D.C.) 62
Wassermann, Jack 39-40

Wenner-Gren, Axel (Wenner-Gren Project) 32
West, Wally 17
Westbank 182
Whitehorse Star (newspaper) 26
Whittacker, Jack 27
Williams Lake 25, 51-52
Williston, Ray 24-26, 63, 68-70, 114-115, 137-139, 154
Wills Variation Act 186
Wine business, in Alberta 78; in B.C. 78, 155-156, 160, 178-179, 181; in Ont. 146
Winnipeg (Man.) 6, 17, 59, 76, 80, 95, 141, 148-150, 168, 170, 180, 183
Wisconsin (Milwaukee) 142
Wolyn (Russia) 1
Women, in labour force 97; Ginter as "womanizer" 99-100, 188
Woodward's (store) 55
Workers Compensation Board 177
World War II 1, 3-4, 7, 15, 32
Yellowhead Highway 33
Yukon 26 (Whitehorse), 51, 131
Zapf, Lloyd 149, 182
Zarek, Eugene 110, 117, 125-126, 132, 138

Material for this book was obtained from the College of New Caledonia, interviews with numerous individuals who had known or worked for Ben Ginter, as well as from Canadian Press, and the following publications: *The Prince George Citizen, The Vancouver Sun, The Province, The Canadian Magazine, The Prospect,* and *The North Star.* Much of the material was drawn from notes I had made while working for *The Prince George Citizen.*

Photos are courtesy of Mrs. Grace Ginter, The Fraser Fort George Regional Museum, Dave Milne, Lorne Lloyd, and Murray Swanson.